YOU TOO CAN SUCCEED

Books by the Author

On Self-Improvement and Success

Make a Way Where There is None

50 Days to Top

Be the Best

Ways of Success and Happiness

Yes You Can

Without Fear and Favour – An Autobiography

Other Books

Some Untold Tales

The Indian Kaleidoscope

Inside CBI

Outside CBI

Inside India

Inside Indian Police

Good Governance

Born to Win

Belling the Cat

Discovery of Independent India

What others have to say about the author's earlier books

... was an eye-opener.

– *The Times of India*

... is an excellent prescription for the young and growing not only on how to succeed but also how to achieve excellence.

– *M L Khanna*
Gen Sec, DAV College Managing Committee

... will be a source of great inspiration and instill courage in the youth and make them strive for their best to succeed. The book is very commendable.

The Hindu

YOU TOO CAN SUCCEED

Joginder Singh
IPS (Retd.)

NEW DAWN PRESS, INC.
UK • USA • INDIA

NEW DAWN PRESS GROUP

Published by New Dawn Press Group

New Dawn Press, 2 Tintern Close, Slough, Berkshire, SL1-2TB, UK
e-mail : ndpuk@mail.newdawnpress.com

New Dawn Press, Inc., 244 South Randall Rd # 90, Elgin, IL 60123, USA
e-mail: sales@newdawnpress.com

New Dawn Press (An Imprint of Sterling Publishers (P) Ltd.)
A-59, Okhla Industrial Area, Phase-II, New Delhi-110020, India
e-mail : info@sterlingpublishers.com
www.sterlingpublishers.com

You Too Can Succeed
© 2004, Joginder Singh
ISBN 1 845570 68 5

All rights are reserved. No part of this publication may be reproduced, stored in a retrieval system or transmitted, in any form or by any means, mechanical, photocopying, recording or otherwise, without prior written permission of the original publisher.

PRINTED IN INDIA

Preface

A number of books are available on the methods and techniques for excelling in life. They are worth a perusing because each one of them has something worthwhile to say. Life is too short to be wasted. A pill for success has not been invented as yet. Success is like good timber, which does not grow with ease. The stronger the wind, the stronger will be the tree. It is the same with us humans. There are plenty of opportunities all around us. What we need most of the time is perseverance. It is a virtue by which even mediocrity can achieve glorious success.

You can do almost anything if you work and keep on working; if you try and keep on trying. Nothing in this world can replace persistence. Calvin Coolidge says: "Talent will not; nothing is more common than unsuccessful men with talent. Genius will not; unrewarded genius is almost a proverb. Education will not; the world is full of educated derelicts. Persistence and determination alone are omnipotent." If you want to have more than what you have got, you have to become more than what you are. This is possible only if you do your best every day. We should always be willing to stretch beyond our limits, willing to renew our commitment to happiness, to becoming the best we can be. Too often we give up too soon. Sometimes, we don't even bother to try because we are convinced that we will be unsuccessful. It would be interesting to examine why this is so. Is it because we are letting our past experiences dictate our present? Whatever beliefs you are holding about happiness or failure, be willing to get rid of these self-limiting beliefs. You have to be willing to break through your own self-imposed boundaries. Incontrovertible and undeniable victories come as a result of hard labour. No real victory comes cheap and none will in the future. Luck is not merely being in the right place at the right time. In fact, it is an energetic and dynamic process of creating the life you want. Do not just sit back and hope that good things will happen to you. Be courageous and go all out after what you want. Commit yourself to your goal and visualise your success daily. Luck will then "happen" to you. It will come to you when you do what you are meant to do in order to make your dream come true. Do not fall into the category of people who are always talking about the trouble they once had, or the trouble they now have or they expect to have. Instead, believe that yesterday got over last night and today, there is a chance to begin anew. Put the past behind you and move on. True wisdom lies in knowing when and what to overlook and ignore. Do not trap yourselves in the past, including past regrets and past hurts. Do not punish yourself and others for what happened in the past. Instead, do something really brave. Look into the future. Don't look back. Start opening doors to your happiness by opening yourself to its possibility. Start by letting go. Henry David Thoreau, an American thinker has said: "What a man thinks of himself, that is what determines, or rather indicates, his fate."

This book is a small step in helping the readers look ahead and make the best of their lives. Go ahead and enjoy it.

Sector 22, Plot No 4, Flat No 124,   **Joginder Singh**
Nav Sansad Vihar GHCS   *IPS (Retd.)*
New Delhi-110 045
Ph.: 30982921
E-mail:jogindersingh@mantramail.com

Contents

	Preface	v
1.	The Rules of the Game	1
2.	Grow Rich	28
3.	Motivate Your Employees	50
4.	A Recipe for Success	67
5.	Feel Terrific about Yourself	93
6.	The Requirements for Creativity	118
7.	Organise Your Work and Home Life	136
8.	Preparing for Success	157
9.	There Is More than One Way to Success	185
10.	New Year Resolution	205

1
The Rules of the Game

Live by the Rules

If life is a game, then there must be rules which you need to observe to reach the pinnacle of success. Generally, the rules are simple, but are often ignored.

The next time you find yourself criticising someone, ask yourself whether doing so is going to change anything. That person will remain the same. You will only demean yourself, seem small and petty, even in your own eyes. Denigrating another person never built anyone up; it just manifests one's own weaknesses of jealousy, envy, resentment, anger, hatred, or fear.

Generally, people are mean to each other because they are insecure and afraid of not being loved. They protect themselves by making themselves difficult to love. In other words, if somebody feels himself unlovable, he will act unlovable. A person having self-esteem believes that he is lovable and worthy of friendship, and acts accordingly. In short, for developing self esteem, you have to change yourself first and stop worrying about other people's behaviour. The secret of forming long-lasting, positive, and fulfilling relationships is to feel secure yourself. You can give your love and friendship freely only if you yourself are lovable. A worthwhile human being will not permit anybody else to enfeeble his self esteem. In fact, others can weaken your self esteem only if you allow them to. If you have a positive view of your self, you will treat others with respect and kindness. Your relationships with others reflect what you feel about yourself. Make sure to have, and present, a positive manifestation of yourself. Always show yourself at your best. Incidentally, you can determine how confident people are by listening to what they DON'T say about themselves. Their attitude and demeanour speak for them. Here are a few things to consider if you want to make a lasting impression and have a positive influence on others.

Recognise the contradiction. Generally, when we try very hard to make a lasting impression, we do not succeed. We do so when we just live our normal lives and do what may seem like ordinary, commonplace, everyday things. Certainly, there are some people like film stars or actors, or sportsmen, who make an impact through their achievements or by virtue of their celebrity status. But lasting impressions are not reserved only for famous people. We can make such impressions every day, every moment. This is possible in all the roles we play in our lives, whether it be of a child, a husband, a parent, an employee, or a businessman. We must live each moment of our life consciously. Too often, we live our lives on "auto pilot". We live mostly by habit, without realising the impact our actions may have on others. In many of these circumstances, our behaviour does not correspond with our professed values. But it is possible to live on a higher level if we always try to do our best.

One of the most effective and vital inputs to success is successful relationships. No man is an island and nobody gets to the top by himself. We can learn from every person we meet, and in some ways, they may be superior to us. Winston

Churchill, 1874-1965, British statesman and Prime Minister once said: "Personally, I'm always ready to learn, although I do not always like being taught."

We either inspire or are inspired by others. In other words, some people give you confidence; when you are depressed, they encourage you. Then there are others, who pull you down. But only those people become successful who master the art of building up others. One of the key secrets of successful relationships is the ability to inspire and encourage people. One way to build up people is to praise them. There is great power in appreciating people. Something good begins to take place in your relationship when you praise someone.

Recollect a time when someone praised you. It was fantastic, you felt elated and you probably liked that person more after he praised you. Praise and appreciate the happy, hard-working and honest people, and let them know how much you admire them. You can do this with a word, or a card, or a phone call. Choose a quality to praise. Suppose there is a dedicated worker in the office. You can say something like this: "It appears that you are always the first one to arrive at the office and the last one to leave. You really set a good example. It is wonderful to have such a hard worker as a boss (colleague or subordinate, as the case may be)."

We should not praise people just for the sake of praising. We should honestly look for positive traits in the character and actions of the people around us. Lying to people should not be a part of this exercise. If somebody has done something wrong, tell him, but while doing so, also say something appropriate in the form of praise. You will see the benefits in the way your relationship will improve. Life is all about associations and relationships, with family, friends, and co-workers. When we praise people for their positive qualities, our relationships grow. It puts our relationships on a fast track, leading to a growth in our influence. Greater leadership and influencing capacity are possible only by helping to improve the lives of people, rather than demeaning them. Abraham Lincoln, 1810-1865, the sixteenth President of the USA once said: "I am a slow walker, but I never walk backwards."

When you appreciate and praise others, they become fiercely loyal, as they realise that you care for them, love them, and appreciate them. This approach will help in your path to success.

Have a grand vision

Two of the most difficult barriers to your peace of mind are discouragement and pride. Discouragement overtakes us when we fail to achieve our goals, or when we are too tired, or indifferent, or sick, or in debt, and feel that there is no meaning or purpose in our life. This happens due to our lack of vision of the big picture, when we face failure and frustration and are afraid. Discouragement is simply lack of courage. It is the result of meandering without a route map in life and building our lives on illusions instead of principles. Discouragement is like being lost in the woods without a compass or an accurate map. It is something which our acquaintances and friends inculcate in us by their discouraging and depressing comments and their analysis of our actions. It distracts us from our goals.

Courage, as a quality, can be developed. Courage is the consequence of our achieving our goals, gratifying our needs and using our capacities in a balanced way, with a clear vision. The best way to develop courage is to aim for a goal, and achieve it. If you make a promise, no matter how small, abide by it. This will help in building your confidence. This is the first step to growth, and peace.

Another factor which leads to vacillation and is a major obstacle in our efforts is pride. The word pride is sometimes used to describe deep pleasure or satisfaction towards something or someone, for achieving excellence. It can also be a destructive factor in life. Says C S Lewis: "Pride gets no pleasure out of having something, only out of having more of it than the next man ... It is the comparison that makes you proud; the pleasure of being above the rest ... Pride is a spiritual cancer: it eats up the very possibility of love, of contentment, or even common sense."

Consider the impact of pride in fulfilling our fundamental needs and capacities. Some people feel their pride demands a certain lifestyle, even if it means living above their income. Such people are always comparing their appearance, their clothing, their physique, with others. Some people measure pride by the number and prestige of the friends they think they have, or the praise bestowed on them by others. Such people judge their worth with the above yardstick. Some people are proud of the degrees they have, of how learned they are. They feel that higher education gives them the highest status. However, one should be prepared to appreciate people who are better-looking, who are richer or who have more friends, or a bigger house, or a newer car. Pride should not lead to hate, envy, and conflict.

Some people get their sense of satisfaction and pride by assessing how far up the ladder they are, as compared to others. They do not bother about whether their ladder is leaning against the right wall or not. Pride is devastating to peace of mind. Proud people spend a lot of time and energy worrying over who has the most wealth or the bigger car, or who looks better, or lives in the better part of town, or has the larger office. For them, the call of competition is louder than the whisper of conscience. It upsets their priorities in life. The antidote for pride is humility. We need to realise that no man is an island, that the quality of our lives is linked to the quality of the lives of others. The more we value principles and people, the greater will be our peace of mind.

Sometimes when we articulate a strong desire and act to fulfil it, the results are instantaneous. It is not always a miracle, but the result of our efforts and hard work. There are many imponderables in the world which work for us. We cannot always discover how they interrelate or work together. But the moment we take a decision to create a result, all the forces in the universe revolve and converge to lend a hand for the achievement of our goal. It continues till we achieve the goal, or stop the progression. This is why I say that there is nothing you cannot do. When you really want to, almost anything can be done somehow.

To do great things requires a certain state of mind. It requires optimism, determination, clarity, love for all mankind, and humility. Optimism and hope comprise the resourceful, innovative and worthwhile way to think. If you have faith, and the belief that there will be a way out, the circumstances will enable you to ultimately find it. Determination should be the key to do what is necessary, even if it is not opportune and expedient. Even if you are not in the mood, and even if it takes more than you expected, is not fair, or you have to contribute more than others do, keep on persevering. At the same time, it is essential to have clarity of focus. The clearer your focus, the more compelling your sway and power will be to activate events in your favour. Make it a habit to set your goals in writing. This is essential to get matters going. If you believe unflinchingly in your cause, you will notice that an invisible universal force will draw towards you to make it happen. Contrary to what many may proclaim, greed does not work. Avarice alienates you from others. Only love and respect will attract and hold all those who might ultimately help you. Love for humanity embraces respect for the dignity and sensitivity of others. It is reciprocal, and what you give, will come back to you.

Focus on the positive

Shakespeare says in his play, *Hamlet*: "There is nothing either good or bad, but thinking makes it so." Once there was a king who told his courtiers that two dogs live in his mind, one of which is fearful and angry, the other courageous and joyful. These dogs are embroiled in a constant fight. One of the courtiers asked, "Which dog wins?" The king answered, "The one I feed." This is true for all of us. Every day holds a choice for us. It is for us to focus on either the negative or the positive aspects. Negative thoughts generally generate an ambience of insecurity, fear and cynicism. Positive beliefs and attitudes give a sense of optimism ... The choice is entirely up to us. Generally, people discount this significant fact and believe that actions and events in our lives determine our state of mind and our success or failure in life. According to Richard Carlson, a psychologist, nothing is further from the truth. "It's our thinking about our circumstances, not the circumstances themselves, that determines how we feel." Consider the case of two of my friends who turned fifty. Each had a different interpretation of the event. One of them figured that his life was coming to an end, and began getting his affairs in order. The other man saw his fiftieth birthday as an opportunity to take on a new challenge and decided to try to reach the top in his profession as an exporter. He became a very rich man at sixty-five. It is not the events of our lives but our thoughts that shape who we are today, and who we will be tomorrow. Fortunately, God has given us the power to be able to see the circumstances of our life positively. Any one or a possible combination of the following measures can help in cultivating the habit of focussing on the positive in all situations.

Discover a lesson: If a difficult event occurs in your life, try to discover and perceive a lesson from it. Ask yourself, "What is the lesson for me in this occurrence? How can I make the most of this event to become a better person?" This approach will transform your next challenge into something positive and rewarding. Always be seeking and looking for the wisdom and lessons you can draw from events. This way you will not think of any adverse episode in your life as a catastrophe. Instead, you can benefit, from the occasion if you shift your focus to see every competition as an opportunity for both personal and professional growth.

Take stock: Never encourage or join in any pity party. Instead, use it as an opportunity to focus on the positive. Do not always be lamenting about what is wrong in your life. Many people, if they are unemployed, lament that they have no money and nothing to do. If such people have a job, they lament that they are under stress and never have time for themselves. Some people keep on wallowing endlessly in negative thoughts. Always being miserable and lamenting that life is giving you a raw deal is not much fun. The next time such thoughts overtake you, take a piece of paper and a pen, and make an honest record of the things in your life that make you happy and contented. You will feel peaceful, and grateful to God, because the pleasing and desirable factors in your life will exceed the difficulties and drawbacks. You will discover that it is nearly impossible to be obliged and appreciative, and miserable, at the same time. In fact, studies have shown that it is virtually impossible to feel any negative emotion such as anger, fear or sadness, while at the same time feeling grateful. This simple technique can quickly help you attain a positive state of mind. Learn to think about life in terms of the roses rather than the thorns. If our train or plane is delayed, we focus on the late arrival and are not thankful for the safe journey and safe arrival. We complain about our servants and household work instead of being thankful that we can afford a comfortable home, fully furnished with all conveniences. In other words, when we receive roses, we complain about the thorns which come with them. This is the wrong reaction, but the fact remains that most people look only at the negative and not the positive side. The best approach to life is to look for the good in any situation and enjoy it. Ask yourself the question, "What is good about this situation and how can I relish the goodness?" This approach may not eliminate all your difficulties but it will ensure a happier life. In other words, look for the roses in life and not the thorns. Ask yourself significant questions and your mind will answer them. Generally, questions beginning with "Why" pertain to the past. Your mind can amplify and elucidate the same. A question beginning with "What" can help your mind become creative and resourceful. Says Peter McWilliams: "Our lives are a combination of the good and bad, the positive and negative. When we focus on the good that is already present, we feel better. If not, we don't. Either way, life goes on." Next time you are faced with a challenging assignment, instead of asking yourself: "Why me?" ask yourself what is the best you can do to get the desired outcome. The only way to enhance joy, contentment and happiness in life is to focus on the positive side of all situations. It is a choice that is up to us. Choose hope, cheerfulness and confidence.

Keep the garbage out

There will always be junk floating around, trying to clutter up our minds.

It never ceases to amaze me when people wanting success, actually put trash into their minds and then expect their minds to work at full efficiency, and deliver success. Reflect on what you put into your mind, through reading, listening to, and meeting others. We live in a rapidly changing world and are hard pressed for time. So it is of utmost importance that we do not spend our precious time cluttering up our minds with rubbish. The acid test for this is simple: will the activity you are spending your time on, transform you into a better person and help you in accomplishing your goals or will it drag you down?

A friend who was hard pressed for time found that he was spending a lot of his time watching television. One day, on impulse, he decided to give away his television. He tells me that now he has ample time to do all he ever wanted to. He also says that he does not have to spend a lot of energy in tuning and filtering his mind to success. Find out which activity does not add to your success or career aims. Either reduce it or cut it out altogether. Proper dietary intake and exercise will go a long way towards our mind's ability to tune into success. Do not load the body with food which it cannot absorb or cope with. The right food also stimulates the brain, igniting it to success.

Commitment: *No matter what product or service you are providing or are proposing to provide, a solid commitment, along with fervency, passion and dedication is essential for success.*

Quality: *Ensure that whatever you are doing is of top quality. Your projections or messages about your self and your organisation, should be of the highest quality. Keep in mind, the other's point of view and be consistent in your approach and conduct, to establish your standing and reliability. Consistency is another name for reliability. Seek to astound, amaze and surprise through your performance and efforts. The rapid rate of technological advancement sometimes tricks people into thinking that instant and huge success is possible, like ready-made products in the market. On the contrary, our success comes from building up relationships, hard work and* sleepless toil, and the perception, in other people's minds, about our sincerity.

Rules for Conditioning Your Mind

No one should underrate the power and role of the mind in one's success. But it is critical to keep our minds positive and on the right track if we wish to achieve balanced success in our career, finances, health, emotions, relationships and spiritual lives. There is a tremendous resemblance between our mind and a TV or radio station. The only way you can listen to a radio station or watch TV, is by tuning into it. Without doing so, you cannot receive any signals. The same is true of our mind. If our minds, beliefs, feelings and opinions, are unfocussed, our success will also remain distant. If our minds stay tuned to accomplishment and triumph, all our actions, will lead to the same. The first requirement is to turn the mind into a success station. The following are some suggestions for being success oriented.

One great difference between animals and human beings is that human beings can make choices. They do not always have to live by instincts. Constant practice of preferences builds up our habits. If we are desperate for success, it is bound to come our way. It is just like the exercises, through which we build up our physical stamina and strength. A similar exercise is required for building up the mind and keeping it 'fit'. If you want to keep yourself and your mind success-oriented, it is up to you to keep it healthy by making superb and positive choices and decisions on a consistent basis. For example, you can overcome any bad habit by using your mind, your determination and by making a choice to change. There are just two alternatives: either changing yourself, or staying in the same channel. You can choose to tune your mind to a different station, other than success. Our world is changing on a daily basis. So to respond to changes, we have to stay away from the "We've always done it that way" mindset, and constantly ensure that our efforts are focussed on both short-term and long-term goals, and not on the past. It is important to fill your mind and brain with momentous and significant ideas. Use your natural ability to decide and make the best choices.

There is a lot of material that lodges in our minds and eventually expresses itself in our actions. There are a number of outside influences which we come across every day and a lot of ideas that we put into our minds on purpose. It is up to us to make positive and momentous choices, to put excellent thoughts into our minds, on a regular basis. When you want to put good ideas, into your mind, regularly, ask yourself first, whether it is positive or negative? Will it build you up or pull you down? Will it make a better or lesser person of you? Will it encourage you to grow or stunt your growth? Will it tune your mind to success, make you success-oriented? Will it move you towards your goals in the areas of your life where you want to achieve success?

It is How You Do it that Matters

Low self esteem and insecurity and how they relate to self confidence is an interesting issue. We all recognise what low self esteem and insecurity feel like. *The Penguin Psychology Dictionary* has this to say about self esteem and other similar matters:

Self Esteem*: The degree to which one values oneself.*

Insecurity*: A lack of assurance, uncertainty, unprotectedness.*

Self Confidence*: Assuredness and self reliance*

Self Belief*: Faith in one's intrinsic competence*

Self Love*: Any extreme form of love for oneself*

Self Image: *One's impression of oneself, often unconscious*

All these concepts reflect esteem, and their opposite is "low self-esteem."

However, even for people with high self esteem, there are some questions: Do people with high self esteem value themselves all the time? Do "secure" people never feel uncertain? Does having self confidence mean that you never rely on others? If you have self belief, do you never doubt yourself? Is 'self love' good or bad? Of course everyone feels uncertain at times and on occasions, every one doubts his own abilities. Occasionally you may feel low. But remember nothing lasts for ever and this phase too shall pass. If you think about the times you have really enjoyed yourself, felt particularly calm in a situation, or performed really well, you will find that those were the times when you weren't really aware of yourself at all! Acceptance of yourself will allow you to enjoy doing whatever you need to do.

You have to take action yourself to acquire self esteem. The person who asserts himself and desires self esteem, gets it. It is just like responsibilities gravitating to the person who is willing to shoulder them. Some of us feel that the universe keeps handing us the difficult propositions, while some of our lucky friends have a smooth sailing. You naturally question – why me? The fact is that if you make up your mind, you can handle anything, however difficult it may be, and come out with flying colours.

Each one of us can face life exactly the way it should be done. The only requirement is the necessary strength and courage. Most of us are way too diffident and feel that our strengths and talents are not enough to make a difference to make a positive change in our lives or in the lives of others. This kind of thinking robs you of happiness. Don't ignore your skill and competence. Use them to make your own life and the lives of others better somehow. Each life is intertwined with another life. Make the most of this powerful, exciting connection by doing what you can do, no matter what the circumstances may be. Do not give up, thinking that your input will not be enough. Every little bit counts in life, and so does your share. God has given you strengths and talents for you to use. Otherwise, there would have been no reason for your being blessed with the same. Most of us feel how wonderful, how much easier, life would be if only we could be happy and discard our sorrows and woes. We can have such an existence, provided we have the courage to let go our anger, disappointment, pain, and resentment. We also need courage to forgive ourselves and others, and look upon each day as another chance at happiness regardless of what might have come to pass in the past. You have to let your fears go, and believe that happiness lies ahead. You only need courage to be, to find joy.

Use it or lose it
When Einstein died in 1955, the pathologist removed and kept his brain, without any permission from his family. For the next 40 years, he studied it under microscope. He also gave small pieces to other researchers upon request. The idea behind this was that to uncover the secret of Einstein's genius.

He did not find anything. But in the early 1980s, one of his colleagues, Marian Diamond a neuro-anatomist of the University of California, announced an amazing discovery which revolutionised the ideas about learning and genius.

Making a genius
Most people assume that geniuses are born, not made. Diamond wanted to find out. She obtained sections of Einstein's brain and examined them. As she expected, she found an increased number of glial cells in Einstein's left parietal lobe – a kind of neurological switching station that

Diamond described as an "association area for other association areas in the brain". Glial cells act as a glue, holding the nerve cells together, and also help transfer electrochemical signals between neurons. Diamond expected this because she had also found high concentrations of glial cells in the brains of her enriched rats on whom she had experimented. Their presence in Einstein's brain suggested that a similar enrichment process was at work.

Stimulate your mind

Unlike neurons, which are another type of cells which do not reproduce after birth, glial cells, axons, and dendrite cells can increase in number throughout life, depending upon how you use your brain. Diamond's research work has proved that the more we learn, the more such connections are formed. Likewise, when we cease learning and our minds stagnate, these connections shrivel and dwindle away.

The implications are clear. Einstein himself had some thoughts on the subject. He believed that you could stimulate resourceful and inventive thoughts by allowing your imagination to soar. The only condition being that imagination should be unrestrained by conventional inhibitions. In other words, we should go with the flow and improve our brain power. We are unlikely to be able to alter our God-given intelligence. But we can alter our crystallised intelligence. It is like anything else: we either use it or lose it. We need to do mental gymnastics. Dr Michael Howe, a psychologist from Exeter University, says: "You have to put in the work, even those who people say are natural geniuses – that's not true, they work at their particular skill all the time."

Motivation is central to this activity for development of the brain. Only those who are really motivated can apply themselves hard mentally. Motivation is part of cognitive intelligence and it determines the quality and quantity of mental capacity. According to Professor Sternberg: "Studies show that adults who use their intelligence actively do increase in intelligence". It is up to us to improve our value, competence and aptitude by constant use of our faculties.

The Winning Formula

Better communication is at the heart of achievement and joy. Effective and better communication involves a course wherein you have to give up slang and clichés in your speech. If you are not careful, you may let slangs slip into your everyday speech. Slang merely takes the place of more accurate, descriptive words, and when people cannot find the same, they use slang. To be a good communicator, you need to come up with the real words to say what you mean. Using cliches is like using tried shortcuts around the good vocabulary, of sharper, original, intelligent speech. Words are the building blocks of thought. Avoiding clichés in speech will lead you to avoid them in thinking. A powerful vocabulary enables us to use the right words, which brings desired result. Long, bombastic and unfamiliar words only confound and frustrate those at whom they are directed, either in your letters or messages or conversation. There is no limit to the amount of information you can store in your brain. It has a tremendous capacity to absorb knowledge. You can learn and master anything you want. The brain is vastly superior to any computer. If it is so, what obstructs us in our pursuits?

Most often, we are our own worst enemy. One of the biggest impediments to our acumen and judiciousness is what we secretly believe about ourselves. We all have a little voice in our head, which tells us that we are not smart, and cannot succeed. One of the first steps to self improvement is to rid yourself of all negative thoughts entrenched by the past influence of your parents, teachers, schoolmates and colleagues. The learning process is enhanced when you are in a relaxed yet alert and positive state. This makes it easier for you to assimilate and remember new information and concepts. You have to strive for excellence, and look for methods which will help you improve your problem-solving skills. You can choose impressing others with your encyclopaedic knowledge and putting forth significant argument with facts. You can draw up the neatest and most concise list of arguments in your favour. You can develop skills for solving the problems in new and uncharacteristic ways. For example, if you are comfortable writing things down, you may have to take the verbal approach sometimes. This way, you will get an insight into other useful methods that might work for you.

Researchers at the University of California, San Diego, have discovered that yogic breathing exercises and techniques can improve the way your brain works. The research shows that when you are working with words and logic, your left brain tends to be more active. When you handle images or music, your right brain is more involved. We all have a natural two-hour cycle of switching between the two sides. One of the ways to interrupt the cycle is to breathe through only one nostril – the left makes your right brain dominant and vice versa. So you can fine-tune your brain for a particular task. This may appear simplistic – just closing the appropriate nostril and breathing strongly through the other. Most psychologists lay emphasis on a positive outlook for achieving any objective. Some people, in trying to have a more realistic view of themselves, tend to look negatively at what is likely to happen. However, too much of realism can be a serious drawback, when you want to push through with a new and difficult project. At the same time, one should be realistic enough to have courage and make a detailed assessment of anything one wants to do. If you always use rose-tinted spectacles, you will be more prone to mistakes. Research suggests that response and intellectual are closely linked.

Many people feel that they are condemned to mediocrity and will not amount to anything in life. There are some who question why others have got that they have not. It is important to remember that geniuses seldom distinguish themselves early in their lives. Many have been labelled difficult, slow or even stupid. Thomas Edison, whose record 1,093 patents outstripped every inventor in history and transformed human life, was not a good student in school. "My father thought I was stupid," Edison later recalled, "and I almost decided I must be a dunce."

As a child, Albert Einstein, too, seemed not good enough to his elders. He had difficulty in both speaking and reading. His poor language skills provoked his Greek teacher to tell him, "You will never amount to anything." Only his mother encouraged him and told him that he would be a great man one day. Einstein was expelled from high school. He also failed in his college entrance examination. After finally completing his bachelor's degree, he failed to obtain either an academic appointment or a recommendation from his professors. He was literally forced to accept a lowly job in a Swiss patent office. In his mid-twenties, Einstein seemed fated for a life of mediocrity. But in his twenty-sixth year, he published his Special Theory of Relativity – which contained his famous formula, $E = mc^2$ – in the summer of 1905. Sixteen years later, he won the Nobel Prize and became an international celebrity. It was same with Dr Hargobind Khurana, who failed to get job as a Professor in Punjab University, Chandigarh. After migrating to the USA, he won the Nobel Prize. The present President of India, Dr A P J Abdul Kalam, failed to get an assignment in the Indian Institute of Bangalore as a Professor. Later he was awarded the Bharat Ratna, and found eminently suitable and acceptable as the First citizen of the country. These are the inspiring examples, which show that men can achieve what they strive for.

Get organised for success

Kick-start every day for getting on to the fast track to success. It is important to maintain the motivation level and be focussed, in whatever one is doing. Treat every day as a new year, because each date comes after one year. For some, every day can either be frantic or quiet, depending on their professions: Wise planning is the basis of all achievement, both today and tomorrow and the day after tomorrow. If there is no planning for whatever you want to achieve or goal setting is not done, you will simply be meandering along. This will be a reactive, not a proactive approach. Only when you know where you are going can you take the steps to get there.

Regardless of your job or profession, you need to plan for success and decide where you would want to be, personally and professionally, at the end of this day, this month and this year, and after five or ten years. You must form a habit of the periodical personal stocktaking by asking yourself what you have achieved so far, and where you want to be by the end of year. Ask yourself what skills, courses, or people do you need to help you to reach your goals. List the specific ACTIVITIES, you need to do for reaching your goals. Form the habit of maintaining a planning diary.

This is very important, as you may have the best intentions but if you are not clear about how and when you are going to act, your goals will remain wishful thinking. The same approach is required from a leader in his organisation, for guiding the people working with him. The leader should set up a "big-picture" and determine the long-term goals for his organisation.

John Maxwell says, "Leaders must be close enough to relate to others, but far enough ahead to motivate them." The same principles apply to our personal life. According to Lord Chesterfield, "Character must be kept bright as well as clean."

Nothing will change if you change nothing. In life, it is easier to float along, and if you are just floating, you will get nowhere. Stand up on your own rather than taking the easy option of floating along with the crowd. According to Henry Ford, the hardest work known to 'man' is ... thinking. If circumstances have put obstacles in your way, take time to think and plan, so that by this time next year, you can happily say to yourself that you have succeeded in achieving the goals you set for yourself and have taken control of your life instead of life taking charge of you. The satisfaction attained by setting goals and achieving them will enhance your confidence and encourage you to strive even harder. Only planning, commitment and action can get you where you want to reach in life. Remember, that we can decide our own destiny, good or evil, and what once comes to pass, can never be undone. Every small stroke of virtue or of vice leaves its indelible mark.

When you get your act together, you naturally get your life together. Always try to be in a happy mood. Only when your "To Do List" is empty and your jobs are complete, can you afford to sit down and relax, and take the load off your feet, till you start for your next goal. It will also be a time to reflect on what has gone by, so that you can learn from the experience, and celebrate your highs. This is possible only if your journey in life is smooth and your chosen path clear. Only you can do it, nobody else can. Introspection should be a part of your daily renting. Some people are in the habit of gossiping about others. Ask yourself, as to how does this help you. Question yourself: do you need to change this behaviour and replace it with more positive one, such as saying only positive things behind other people's backs? All of us face difficulties created by others, at one time or the other, in our lives. Ask yourself whether you should try to discuss it with them, or should avoid them. Do you harbour ill feelings towards them? Ask yourself, how you would behave if you were the one creating the difficulties, and what would be the best method of tackling you. You may also question what you need to change about yourself, your beliefs and behaviour in order to have the friendship and level of intimacy that you need in your life while interacting with others? Each problem you solve should became a lesson, which should help you solve other problems later. Any other approach would amount to reinventing the wheel. Happiness is marvellous. The place to be happy is here and the time to be happy is now. One way to be happy is to help others to be happy. It is a two-way street. Every worthwhile achievement in life, whether big or small, has its stages of tough grind and conquest. It has the stages of tough beginning, relentless struggle and final triumph. There is no easy path to magnificence. There is no trouble-free road to eminence. Its rewards demand fighting, endurance and grit. A rugged disposition that will not give up is required to reach eminence.

Take charge of your life

Our success in business, sports, friendship, love, nearly every enterprise we attempt, is largely determined by our own self-worth. People who have confidence in their personal worth are magnets for success and happiness. Good things happen to them regularly. Their associations are long-lasting. They complete all their projects and, as the English poet William Lake says, they "catch joy on the wing".

Conversely, there are people who lack self esteem and become magnets for failure and unhappiness. Their plans go astray. They end up destroying their own potential success and happiness. Nothing seems to work out for them. Their problems usually arise from a difficulty with self-assurance. When such person gains more confidence, his troubles also disappear. Almost any one can change his self-motivation. People with low self esteem should not feel that they are doomed to a life of unhappiness and failure. It is possible to get rid of negative attitudes. It is also possible to acquire healthy confidence and realise one's dreams through the same. The following are some suggestions:

Always focus on your potential for success, on your plus points, and not on your limitations. Refuse to be limited by your limitations. You can do this by encouraging yourself and focussing on your strong points, not on the weak ones. You can succeed anywhere, if you chose to. Don't feel inferior, that you are not as smart or good-looking or witty as others. Probably no habit chips away at our self confidence quite so effectively as that of scrutinising the people around us to see how we compare with them. If you find that someone is indeed smarter, better-looking or wittier, you feel inferior, it diminishes your sense of self-worth. The important thing in life is to be yourself fully, in all ways. We should focus on what we do well. There are a lot of unsuccessful people, who have the potential and talent for doing something well. Their problem is that they have not discovered their natural genius and developed that talent. No top surgeon reaches the top from day one. He has to hone his skills for months and years, endlessly. The refining of expertise is the only correct method to improve performance in any field.

Many of us show only sporadic interest in a discipline, but when the going gets tough, we abandon it. Or when we see others more successful, we become disheartened, and capitulate. There are no short cuts to success. It is the frequent, repetitive and regular sharpening of our skills which will lead to success. Most people find their aptitude and place by trial and error. It has to be remembered that achieving success will, and does take time. Obstacles will come along the way. We should not get dismayed if we find that others are more capable and talented. Usually it is determination that makes the difference, indeed it matters even more than talent.

Visualise yourself as a successful and enterprising person. The negative statements we make to ourselves, which flash across our brain and mind every day comprise our undoing, and lead to a diminished self-image.

Practise an ongoing exercise several times a day for building your self confidence. Visualise yourself as becoming successful. Picture yourself approaching a difficult and challenging task with poise and confidence. Do what outstanding athletes often do. They visualise a move over and over in their minds and see themselves hitting a perfect score. Keep such positive images alive in your mind. Embed them deeply till they become a part of the unconscious. Always expect to succeed. Norman Cousin says: "People are never more insecure than when they become obsessed with their fears at the expense of their dreams."

There is no doubt that if we envision beneficial things happening, they have a way of actually happening. Break away from other people's expectations. It is liberating when we decide to stop being what other people want us to be. You will always feel uncomfortable trying to be something you are not, pretending to be familiar with subjects you know nothing of. You must realise that if you are not an intellectual, you will not succeed as an intellectual or a writer. You can succeed only as yourself. A better strategy would be to listen and ask questions, instead of trying to impress others. When you speak, try to contribute, and not always to outshine others. You would feel a new warmth in your social contacts. People will like the real you better. Most of us have a natural inclination in a certain direction. We can discover it by our own instincts. It is up to each one of us to discover this God-given talent. Resisting conformity and developing some qualities are the steps to independence and self confidence.

Building a network of supportive relationships is a great confidence boosting step. Most people try to enhance their self-image with various techniques, but overlook the very source from which they can get help. This source lies within each one of us.

One of the surest ways to improve your self confidence is to make certain you have lots of love in your life. Loving relationships are always confidence building. Love is a two way street. When you give love, it comes back to you. You should go to whatever lengths are necessary to establish a network of sustaining and nurturing relationships. You do not always need to do them, by meeting new people. A better way is to deepen the friendships you presently have. All relationships are a mixed bag. None is totally black or white. Different people have different talents and this is not to be our concern. Our responsibility is to make the best use of our own talents and develop them to the full. It is not important that we have limitations. The important thing is that we should learn to capitalise on the talents we have. Self confidence, like happiness, is capricious when we set out to grab it for its own sake. Usually it comes as a by product of whatever we do. It comes in our service or work, or friendship or love. Suddenly, when we least expect it, one day we realise that we are confident and happy

We should assume responsibility for ourselves. Though time heals all wounds, many people do not recover fully from a crisis despite the expected healing of time. It is important, to deal dynamically with painful experiences like illness, death, divorce or loss of a job, which are inevitable in life. Some people cope by blaming God, or Fate or their colleagues or relatives. The truth is: ultimately we have to assume responsibility for ourselves and our lives. The ability to make a decision and act on it is the secret of a good manager. It is also the mark of anyone who is willing to take risks to achieve his objective and aim in life. We should move beyond our hurt and make something of our lives. We should go in for making tough choices.

No Rule for Success Works, Unless You Do

There are few crucial things in the lives of most of us: job, relationship with the family, health, and wealth. Apart from these, there are some other things that matter immediately in life or on a daily basis. It is important to distinguish between that which is pressing, and that which is important. The important concern is to make the most of life. But more important than that is to act on what you learn. Time management is very important and should be practised. More important than the speed is the destination where you are finally headed. It is up to each one of us to discover for herself/ himself what destination we are heading for and what is important or urgent in our life. Nobody else can do it for us. It is sometimes difficult to distinguish between our commitments – meetings, activities and aims – and what really matters. Most of the time, we are only doing fire-fighting. We are only responding to situations or other people. In the pressure of events, the most significant things in life are either neglected or forgotten. What and how you do it, depends on how competent you are. Says James Allen: "The within is ceaselessly becoming the without ... From the state of a man's heart, proceed the conditions of his life; his thoughts blossom into deeds, and his deeds bear the fruitage of character and destiny."

Says Charles Hummel: "The important task rarely must be done today, or even this week ... The urgent task calls for instant action ... The momentary appeal of these tasks, seems irresistible and important, and they devour our energy. But in the light of time's perspective, their deceptive prominence fades; with a sense of loss, we recall the vital task we pushed aside. We realise, we've become slave of the tyranny of the urgent." It is often that urgency that drives us, at the cost of the things that matter in life. Many times we find it difficult to distinguish between the two or even to decide what is most important.

For fulfilling our needs, it is equally essential to have a good quality of life. That itself is dependent on a number of factors like financial security, good health, energy, education, and competence. Lack of any of the above qualities can affect your life. Any unmet need can adversely affect your health and span of concentration. Everybody has his own aim of self fulfillment. George Bernard Shaw has said: *"This is the true joy of life ... Being used, for a purpose, recognised by yourself as a mighty one ... Being a force of Nature, instead of feverish selfish little clod of ailments and grievances, complaining that the world will not devote itself to making you happy. I am of the opinion, that my life belongs to the whole community and as long as I live, it is my privilege to do for it whatever I can. I want to be thoroughly used up when I die. For the harder I work, the more I live. I rejoice in life for its own sake. Life is no brief candle to me. It is a sort of splendid torch which I have got to hold up for the moment and I want to make it burn as brightly as possible."*

For success, one of the most important inputs is, to decide the most important task or the tasks to be done. Once a consultant offered the following advice for making better use of time, "Write down the six most important tasks that you have to do tomorrow. Number them by importance. First thing tomorrow morning, look at item one and start working on it until you finish it. Then do item two, and so on until quitting time. Don't be concerned if you have not finished them all. Try this system on every working day." I have tried this system personally and I can testify that it works simply gloriously.

Another tip for success is to dress for success. Don't postpone being well dressed till you become successful. More important than what you wear is how you wear your clothes. Clothes are a visible status symbol. They are a worthwhile investment. A poorly dressed person singles himself out as a failure. Carefully fitted clothes are worth the time and money they need. As a person dedicated to achieving success, you should not appear crumpled or sweaty. You should always dress as if you are expecting to be promoted on that basis. Your clothes should give you an image of being a cool, confident and unruffled person. You should enjoy the pleasures and privileges that the journey to success and success itself bring. One of the major obstacles to success is the problem of appropriate clothes. It has to be remembered that people resent sloppiness and react strongly against it. So if you want to succeed, you should show the same not only in your bearing, but also in your clothes. You should look as if you are already successful. Success in any segment is not possible unless you establish a clearly defined goal for which you are working. It may be a top job in your organisation or making more money, winning laurels in writing or any other sphere. You should list your thoughts and goals for each day by spending at least 15 to 20 minutes a day on this. In this period, apart from setting the day's goals, you should also check how many important items of work, listed the previous day, have been completed. Your main goal of life should be inscribed on your mind everyday. You should remind yourself that all your efforts and energies are to be channelled for achieving the same.

2
Grow Rich

The Law of Accretion

One of the greatest principles of success is called the Law of Accretion or Accumulation. This law states that any worthwhile achievement in the history of human life is the result of myriad efforts and sacrifices, big and small, that have mostly gone unseen and unappreciated. It also declares that everything builds up, both consciously and unconsciously, over a period of time. We can see in our own lives that we have to put in great effort, labour and pain that are hardly noticed or appreciated before any achievement comes our way. Our efforts for any accomplishments are like a snowball, which starts small, but grows as it adds millions of minuscule snowflakes. It grows bigger and bigger as it gathers momentum.

Become skilled at what you need to learn

The knowledge about our body by medical science is an outcome of hundreds and thousands of small pieces of information, gathered by painstaking research over centuries. For gathering a large knowledge base, one has to spend thousands of hours building that edifice. It can be done one piece at a time. Experts are valued for their knowledge. But before becoming an expert, that individual has to labour to acquire the high level of knowledge that makes him valuable.

Save your money

Every large fortune is built on the accumulation of hundreds and thousands of tiny amounts of cash. In fact, a number of banks in South Canara (or Mangalore) in Karnataka State, were started on the principle of collecting five or ten rupees every day from small earners. Along with the growth of banks, the small savers, over a period of time, have become millionaires. The place and time to start saving money is to begin now, and form a regular habit of saving. When you begin to save money, it will start a chain reaction and you will be attracted to saving as a regular feature. This will enable you to become a regular saver of money and here the law of accumulation of riches will work to your advantage.

Entice wealth into your life

All those who have become rich will tell you that as soon as you start saving, this habit will attract into your life and into your work all the money that you need to achieve your goals. If you put the initial savings aside to start with from today, you will never retire poor.

Get the wisdom and learning you need

Another relevant area where the law of accretion or accumulation applies is the area of experience. There is no substitute for experience and the most successful people in any domain are those who have far more experiences in that field than an average individual. In business or entrepreneurship or management or parenting or selling or anything else what count are experience, knowledge and skill. Unless a person takes the risks that are necessary to move out of his comfort zone, he will not gain the requisite experience to become successful. Be ready to take risks, do not be afraid that things will not work out. This is a hard but sure way to acquire expertise, ability and proficiency.

Every idea and initiative counts

You cannot grow and become capable of earning the kind of money that you desire unless you move out of the comfort zone and gain experience. Mistakes are the price of experience, and experience is the key to the law of accumulation. Everything, including mistakes, and what you do, counts. The biggest mistake that some people make is the feeling that it is only their opinions or views that are important. When you meet a person and discuss something or read a book, when you listen to music or watch a movie and learn something from all these things, it all counts. No experience in life in any direction is a waste. Our effort should be to learn from it, to convert a minus into a plus.

Use your time positively and constructively

Your effort should be to use time constructively and in such a way that it counts on the plus side. Even if you watch television, waste time, hang out, fool around, it does count, but on the negative side. You can have a great life by the law of accrual and addition, by accumulating more on the credit side than on the debit side. If you have more negatives on the debit side, then you will not move towards your goals. In fact, in that case, you will be moving away from your goals. Whatever you do either moves you towards the things you want in your life, or the person you want to be, or the wealth you want to accumulate, or it causes you to shift away. Everything counts and matters as per the law of accumulation. Starting today, build a strong base about your knowledge in the subject that can be most helpful to you in achieving economic emancipation and autonomy. It may take weeks, months or years to acquire that thorough knowledge. It does not matter. What matters is to just get started today. Whatever your field, do your best to acquire the maximum experience. Make a beginning by starting earlier, working harder, and staying on your job later than others do. Be always open to taking risks and try innovative ways to achieve your goal. This invaluable experience will accumulate over a period of time and will yield rich dividends. If you find that erstwhile theories for achieving success have not yielded the results in your case, you lose nothing by being innovative. On the contrary, you may achieve professional and personal success and realise your cherished dream. Success can be yours, only if you will: It might be at the next corner of your effort.

How to Communicate and Save Money

I have noticed that one of the biggest challenges the business world faces is lack of communication. This is equally true even with family members. I have seen government organisations spending a fortune on purchasing office buildings, but they do not spend on the right furniture, computer software, filing systems or methods of working. This happens because the people using the equipment are never consulted about what their needs or the needs of members of the public visiting them are. To be able to effectively deliver results, in both the government and private sectors, it is vital to keep the communication lines open with the people who are expected to deliver the results, as well as the kind of image you want your organisation to have. A comfortable environment, with appropriate furniture and illumination is very important for delivering results. If new technology demands new skills, it is important to march with the time, and equip the workers with the necessary wherewithal, so that it is in consonance with the image the organisation wants to project. Being in communication with your team has several advantages, and good feedback can help the organisation plan for the necessary changes. It does not always pay to have excellent and grandiose plans. It is equally important to look into the small things, such as whether the furniture is causing health problems, sore backs, eye strain, neck problems and sore wrists. A small work area where one is unable to sit face-on to the computer screen can cause cramps. The solution could be to have work-friendly furniture, where one could sit face-on. With the rapid changes taking place all over the world, organisations have to remember that their people are the biggest asset. It is people who use the machines. Machines do not use people. So talk to your team to find out what their problems are and the possible solutions, in their perception. You can have an in-house written feedback sheet. Do not ask them to sign it, as some may be too scared to complain. Ask them questions, and LISTEN to them. Stop looking for the solutions to your problems elsewhere. First put your own house in order. You may save a lot of money. Working with people is not like an assembly production line, as each human being is different and all have very different needs and inclinations.

Stick to Your Family Budget

There are two ways to get rich. One is to earn more money and the other is to save it. Saving money is very important for achieving your goals. Everybody has to pay a price to make his or her goals a reality. It is a fact that only that team wins, which has, not only a strong desire to win, but is willing to pay the price to win. Many people go only to the extent of desiring something. They get cold feet, when they realise that a price has to be paid. This can create a problem. Putting in extra effort for promotion can in some cases, involve talking to your spouse, as he or she may be unconsciously sabotaging your efforts to concentrate on your work. It can also mean, neglecting a few errands at home. We should expect obstacles, and also be willing to pay the price for the reward. A simple, hopeful approach can have a powerful impact on your life. If you wish to save money, the foremost thing to do is to prepare a financial plan. A financial plan or budget is an estimate of your expected income and expenditure. It is essential that the entire family works on the plan as a composite team. A great deal of discussion is necessary in the family, so that individual disagreements can be voiced and common goals recognised and acknowledged. Each member must implement money control for achieve the plan to succeed.

Each person in the family, including children, should be assigned a personal allowance. This allowance is for personal use and the person given such an allowance, need not account for it. Nevertheless, it is a prerequisite to be realistic about the needs and demands of such pocket money. It also depends upon what the family can afford. The first priority of the family should be to purchase basic common needs before assigning any allowance.

For managing finances well, it is essential to establish the habit of planning ahead, after taking into account both long-term and short-term goals and needs. It is a good, financial management policy to take advantage of special sale prices on planned purchases, whenever an opportunity occurs. At times, you can effect savings of as much as 20 to 25 per cent. For this, it is essential to be well informed about the market situation, the availability and prices of products, including seasonal fluctuations, and where you can take advantage of the same. Sound and good value shopping is possible, only if you do window shopping or pre-shopping research. In a course in the UK, in the University of Manchester, which I attended on best marketing practices, we were advised to look around, compare the prices and quality and then invest our money. Shopping habits should aim at the best buy, at competitive rates. This will make your money go far.

Be careful as some shops in India permanently display discount boards, of up to 50 per cent. You must be wary of them, as they hike up the prices by 100 per cent and then give a discount of 50 per cent on the increased price. Some stores sell items at a discount. The discounted price should be verified before rushing to such shops. Market surveys should become a habit. Once you buy goods, use the same appropriately. Take care of your goods to get the maximum service with a minimum of repair and maintenance costs.

Use your aptitude, skill, capabilities and time to perform as many repairs, overhauls, and checks as possible at home, rather than paying for them. If at all you use credit, then use it wisely and keep credit costs to a minimum. Never become a slave to brand names or labels, or so-called prestige stores. You should always evaluate the quality of the products you buy against the price. Public parks, libraries and services are available at minimal or no cost. Use these to your advantage. There are a plenty of cheats around who will take advantage of you if you are not careful. So always be alert to fraud. Be aware of your consumer rights and responsibilities in the selection, purchase and use of goods and services.

Unwise and indiscreet consumer habits can cause loss of 5 to 25 per cent of your spending amount. Do not hesitate to negotiate, if you feel you are being overcharged. After all, it is your money. You have every right to safeguard your interests, and pay what you consider is a fair price. You are entitled to a fair bargain. It is up to you to make sure that no one takes you for a ride. Identify and avoid wasteful habits such as buying convenience or luxury items which you are not going to use or buying things in excessive quantity. Don't spend on an impulse, or discard belongings and assets which can still be used.

Plan your actual monthly spending against your budget to show whether you and your family are overspending or sticking to the budget. Stick the budget scheme on some prominent place like the fridge door. This should serve as a target for the family as a whole.

Tips for successful negotiation

The ability to negotiate successfully is a crucial element for both success and survival. Negotiation is the solid base on which you build success. You have to keep honing your skills of negotiation on a continuous basis. It is said that everything is negotiable up to a certain point. Successful negotiators are self-assured and forward looking. They do not take things at face value. They think and believe that they have the right to question any asking price. One of my friends who is a very practical man, wanted to purchase a flat in Gurgaon and the asking price of that was Rs. 99 lakhs. He offered Rs. 50 lakhs. The seller jumped as if he had committed a blasphemy. He was shouted at and told that he was not dealing in a vegetable market. At this, my friend Narinder replied that he had every right to quote what he thought was a realistic price. The seller then brought down the price to Rs. 58 lakhs, a steep fall of Rs. 41 lakhs. My friend, who was now in no mood to spend anything, rejected the offer on the ground that the seller had spoiled his mood and he had no intention of doing business with such a person. He told me that he was under no obligation not to question the asking price. He had already made some inquiries and found out the value of real estate in that area. If you want to be a successful negotiator, you should be willing to challenge the validity of the opposite perspective.

A successful negotiator does not believe everything he is told. He is assertive, in the sense that he is clear in his own mind. He is very clear about what he wants and to what extent he is willing to go to convert a "no" to "yes". Each one of us can become a successful negotiator by practising the expression of feelings without anxiety or anger. The trick is to negotiate in a non-threatening way. Express your feelings as if you want to say something, from your point of view, instead of condemning others. Instead of telling a teenager "You shouldn't do that," try saying, "I will be happy if you act in a particular way, or I don't feel comfortable when you do that."

There is a tremendous difference between being assertive, and being antagonistic and belligerent. There is no harm in being determined and resolute, when taking care of your own interests. But at the same time, be respectful of the interests of others. Do not promote your own interests with a lack of regard for other people's interests. If you do so, you are being aggressive. Being vigorous and persuasive at the same time is a part of the negotiation process.

Be a good listener

Good negotiators should be like detectives who can discover hidden meanings by asking probing questions, without revealing anything themselves. The other party, at the negotiating table, will tell you everything you need to know if you just listen. Many differences, disputes and discords can be worked out and disentangled easily if we just listen. Unfortunately, listening has become a forgotten art. Most of us are so busy having our own way that we forget to listen to what others have to say. It would be ideal for most negotiators if they could become effective listeners. They should allow others to do most of the talking, say for 80 per cent of the time. Follow the 80/20 rule. This means, listening 80 per cent of the time and speaking only 20 per cent of the time. Ask open-ended questions, which should be difficult to answer with a simple "yes" or "no."

Prepare yourself thoroughly

Gather as much information as possible, which should be relatable, relevant and significant, about the opposite party involved in the negotiations. It could include their needs, pressure points which can work on them, and their options. It should be done prior to the start of negotiations. Diligent homework is both basic and vital to successful negotiations.

Aim high

A high aim yields high results. People who aim higher, do better. If you expect more, you shall get more. It is equally important for successful negotiators to be optimistic. A proven tactic for achieving superior results is opening the negotiations with an ambitious or extravagant stand. In other words, if somebody is selling something, he should ask for more than he expects to receive. In a similar way, the buyers should offer substantially less than they are prepared to pay. Help the other side feel pleased, content and happily fulfilled by thinking they got what they wanted. Satisfaction means that their bottom lines and basic interests have met. Let there be no confusion about your basic interests and positions. The position is what a negotiator expects or says he wants. The basic interest is their bottom line and what they must pull off. A good negotiator needs to be patient, and not just wanting to get it over with. Whoever is more adaptable, accommodating, and patient, with plenty of time at his disposal, will have an upper edge in negotiations. Impatience can be devastating for the negotiating party which is in a hurry. It is a wise policy in negotiation not to make the first move and let the other party open first. This will enable you to gauge the aspirations of the opponent. You will discover whether his or her expectations are low or high in the ensuing negotiations. It is quite possible that he may agree to less than what you are prepared to offer. On the contrary, if you open the negotiations first, you may give away more than what the other party would have willingly accepted. This way, you would have given more than necessary. As a matter of principle, never accept the first offer. If you do, the other negotiator may think that he could have done better or that it was too easy. Most negotiators will consider it in order, if you reject the first offer. It will give you elbow room to examine the proposal for a better deal. So when you eventually say "yes", you will be giving the impression that you stood pushed to your limit and have done a favour to the other negotiating party. Never make unilateral allowances or concessions or compromises. If you give something away, get something in return. Always do things in sequence and on a reciprocal basis – I'll do this if you do that favour for me. Otherwise, you will give the other negotiator the chance to ask for more.

Never negotiate without alternative selections, choices or preferences. If you depend too much on the positive outcome of a negotiation, you lose the capability and capacity to say "no". If necessary do not hesitate to walk away if the minimum you expect is not forthcoming.

There are no guarantees

The following story appeared in the *Washington Post* about four members of the Forbes 400 list of 2001: "Four of last year's billionaires were wiped out entirely – Swiss shareholder activist Martin Ebner, German media tycoon Leo Kirch, Brazilian television mogul Roberto Marinho and Turkish banker Mehmet Karamehmet." Is it not amazing that in one year a person has a billion dollars and the next year, it is all gone. It means that your one million or billion could go any time, if you are not careful.

We need to appreciate that there are no guarantees in life. We should hold on to all things with a loose grip. If you hold something very hard, it will be more difficult for you when it disappears. Wealth and achievement are fine and should be pursued, and secured. Remember, easy come, easy go.

Our perspective in life should include putting in our best efforts and giving our life everything we have. Strive to achieve your dreams and in the pursuit do not hold back. Enjoy the things you have, whether it is wealth or any achievement. Money and achievements are not necessarily the best things of life. They are merely the means to an end, not the ends themselves. The true riches of life are your peace of mind which you get from people, your friends and family, your character and your faith. Give these the proper place they deserve. For example, do not sacrifice your peace of mind and your family to get wealth. You need your family even when there is no wealth. When you achieve success, share it with your family, friends and others. Be realistic and think about how those four billionaires lost their wealth. There are no guarantees in this life. Circumstances and people can change. Live each day as though it is your last. Enjoy it to the fullest and, at the same time, have plans ready for tomorrow. If good things come, enjoy them. If bad days come, be ready to face them. Good and bad times are all part of life and its processes. Always encourage and cheer yourself, whatever the conditions.

Have the Will to Succeed

Self-belief, self-recognition and self-improvement commence from the time we become aware of the strength, might and influence of our environment, our colleagues, parents and other people with whom we come in social contact. Our own level of self-worth is decided largely by how well we are recognised and acknowledged in our business and social circles. Even our attitude towards ourselves is determined largely by the behaviour and attitude of our peer and social groups. When you believe that others think highly of you, your level of self-recognition and self esteem gets enhanced. The best way to build and have a healthy personality is to have high self esteem.

We should get rid of negative thoughts and influences from our lives. At the same time, we should discard thoughts and feelings which make us feel guilty or ashamed about what has happened in the past and our role in the same. Write down everything and unveil to yourself the sources, causes and sequences of the events. This way you can truly understand what your role has been and how responsible for the event you are, and also what you can do to prevent such incidents in future.

Self-disclosure, and self-awareness can make you aware of your feelings and help you in developing a detached perspective. This way you can evaluate your own thoughts and feelings independently and become more aware of your personality. Ultimately, for happiness and success, every person must learn to accept himself for whatever he is. Each one of us has some good points and some bad points, some strengths and some weaknesses. Your real strength lies in developing the ability to stand back and look at yourself, frankly and objectively. This way you can develop the grit and strength to achieve your goals and enjoy tremendous self esteem and a heightened sense of self-acceptance.

Prepare an inventory of your accomplishments

Make a list of your talents and abilities. Underscore the positive and minimise the negative qualities of your personality and life. Recapitulate your most important skills, and the things that you have completed or can accomplish exceptionally well and successfully, in your profession and/or in your personal life.

The idea is that you encourage yourself, both for your present and your future, and enhance the possibilities for advancement. The fact is that our potential for any achievement we set our heart on is virtually unlimited. We can achieve whatever we want to achieve, do whatever we want to do in life, reach any level we wish for in life and become whatever we want to become. It is up to us to set big or small goals and formulate plans and move step-by-step, progressively towards their realisation. All the impediments are mostly in your mind. There are no hurdles that you cannot overcome.

If something is bothering you and causing unhappiness sit down with your spouse, or a confidante and tell him or her about it. Misery shared is misery halved and discussing your problem with others can help you in developing a perspective on it. Another technique is to get detached from your problem and visualise it as something happening to someone else. Envisage what advice you would give to that person to get over his difficulties. Encourage yourself unremittingly and persistently by thinking about your happy experiences and accomplishments in the past. At all times, think well of yourself. This way, you will attain whatever you want to achieve. There is no limit to what you can bring about in your life. It is really and truly possible that each one of us can resolve any difficulty.

Do not use the so-called realism as a cloak for pessimism. Fortune smiles on those who are committed to a goal. Commitment brings the elements of the universe together in an unlimited and unconstrained way to help you reach your objective. Sometimes we accidently run into a person who helps us to solve our problems. Discontentment in our life arises from ignorance about our capabilities. Most people underestimate their power about what they could do, if they really decided to do something. If you decide, and commit in earnest for a certain outcome, the elements in the entire universe will help you to make it happen. It is the persistence of your faith that starts the inexplicable process. Disbelief, mistrust, suspicion, disgust, and repulsion stop the path of progress. The mind truly tends to bring about what you want it to achieve or do. Hence, always be positive in your approach, whatever the conditions or circumstances.

First Things Should Be Done First

The power of goals is tremendous. Without following the right principles, it is difficult, if not impossible, to do the right thing, even if, for doing the same, you have the right reasons. Only the correct principles can ensure that you succeed in whatever you want to accomplish. Unless you know what you want to accomplish as long-term, short-term, daily, monthly, personal, organisational, ten-year, or lifetime goals, there is no way you can do anything worthwhile. As far as possible, the goals should be measurable, specific and time-bound. Goal setting, as a powerful process, is based on the principle of focus that encourages us to concentrate. It is just like converging the rays of the sun into a force strong enough to start a fire.

If you do not take the right approach and do not succeed, cynicism will follow. These situations obstruct our power of setting and achieving goals. When we meet critical ordeals in our lives, we lack strength and energy for overcoming them. Generally, experiences and feelings about goals are mixed. Some of us can set heroic goals, and exercise tremendous discipline. Some are willing to pay an incredible price for achievement. Others cannot resist even sumptuous food in the interest of their diet and health. Generally, goals are the primary factors in shaping the destiny of individuals and nations. However, some see goals as an ideal that has no staying power in the "real" world. But the fact remains, unless you know where you are going or want to go, you will never get there. So it is better to stick to a goal, no matter how high the price. But nobody succeeds all the time. We should be ready to take the blow to our commitment, dedication, persistence and courage when we do not achieve our goals in the first instance and meet some distressing consequences.

Each one of us has a "Personal Integrity Deposit Recognition Account" maintained in our conscience and personality bank. This account contains the surplus or deficit of the trust we have in our competence and ourselves. When we make and honour our commitments, in respect to other individuals as well as in setting and achieving goals, we make deposits. This increases our confidence in our own reliability, in our ability to make and maintain commitments to ourselves and to others. Having a high balance in this account is a great source of power and potency.

Failure to achieve our goals, is a source of great distress and affects our own standing in our own eyes. It is tantamount to a withdrawal from our self-confidence in our account. Over time, frequent withdrawals cause us to lose confidence in our ability and make us diffident about whether we can make and keep commitments and win our own as well as others' confidence. Scepticism and pessimism follow, affecting our power of setting and achieving meaningful goals. So when we most need strength of character to meet critical conflicts in our lives, we find it missing.

Building a strong character is just like developing physical strength. When the trial comes, if you do not have the strength of character, no make-up can disguise the fact that it is just not there. You cannot fake strength of character. It takes strength to set a goal, as well as to work on knotty problems. A "quick fix" does not work to honour your commitments when the tide of public opinion turns against your accepted values.

There can be many reasons, why we fail to achieve our goals. One reason could be that sometimes the goals we set are unrealistic. We create expectations in our own mind or in the minds of others that do not reflect any sense of self-awareness of our own qualifications or competence. It happens every year, when on New Year's day people expect to change for the better, either in their food or exercising habits or in their conduct with others. Nothing will suddenly change because the calendar shows January 1 instead of December 31. It is like expecting a one day old child to learn to crawl, eat with a fork, and drive a car all on the same day. Our ambitions and targets are based on delusion, with little self-assurance or consideration for the principles of natural growth.

Sometimes when we set goals and work to achieve them, either the circumstances change or we do. A new opportunity comes up which appears better or another person throws light on the problem and reveals it in a different perspective. Holding onto our goals in such circumstances becomes counter-productive. If we can change our goals, it may make us feel better. But it may also make us feel uncomfortable, troubled and uneasy and lower ourselves in our own estimation for not being able to do what we had set out to.

Sometimes, the outcome of end results is at the expense of other more important things in our lives. We have to maintain a balance in our lives, so that in the process of achieving goals, we do not lose our peace of mind. Never do anything or achieve any goal at the cost of a positive attitude, your dreams or your conscience. Our effort should be to put first things first. A man with positive attitude always draw security from inner self.

Turning points

Each decision we take is an important one in its own context, though at times it may appear insignificant. The truth is that all the decisions taken by us add up to become habits. It is these habits which decide our destiny. Sometimes our options mysteriously become real turnouts. Accomplishing first things first makes all the difference to the achievement or quality of life we or our nations lead. Sometimes such decisions are harsh, hard hitting, unpopular and dangerous. But if you listen to your conscience, you will rarely go wrong.

Clear the Clutter

Have a schedule for every activity in your life. One ongoing activity should always be clearing the clutter. How you treat your place, whether it is your home or your workplace indicates how you feel about yourself. A well maintained place generally increases your confidence in yourself. It also enhances your chances of doing things well. Most of us routinely postpone things like cleaning out our wardrobe or getting rid of all that we have not used or worn in the last couple of years. My cousin's wife, Vandana Babbar, told me that when she looked at her store, she realised that she already had a number of items which she wanted to buy, thinking that she did not have them.

I have seen new cars full of rubbish, including glasses, papers, and old clothes that should not be there. Clearing up things can leave you feeling sharp, energised and well organised. To get anything done, it is best to clear the mess and get yourself organised, as clutter drains energy. By sheer inertia, we let things remain as they are and let clutter rule our lives. If your car or working place is a mess, with clutter strewn all over the place, then it is a sure indication that you are off the track. If you are "off the track", ask yourself whether the clutter is overwhelming you and whether it is time to clean up your life? If the answer is YES, then it is time, you did something about it by *taking action*.

Always be punctual, even if there is nobody around to appreciate it. Do not live your life as if you are on a train, believing that happiness is at the next station, the next stage in your life ... to a bigger college ... when you graduate ... get a job ... get married ... get back from the honeymoon ... have children ...when they have grown up and started their own families ... on retirement. Be thankful for what you have at present. Most people fail to understand that happiness is not some distant destination. It is a way of living, a way of existence or a way of being. It is already inside us. Happiness is where we are now. The only requirement is that we have to seize it and make it our own. There is a finishing line at the end of a race. But there is no finishing line that marks that you have arrived at, or beyond, "success".

We all wish to finish our work and be up to date with it. This causes us to worry, about what may happen. The result is that we never live in the present moment. God had a noble mission for all of us and He meant us to become something higher. You have to realise as what you are meant to be, and when you do, you shall become so.

Each one of us can easily achieve goals and get results, by dramatically improving productivity, reducing stress and the mess in life and having more time for living life. The trouble is that most people are too busy being busy. Sometimes, they are busy with almost nothing. You need to focus on your goals, with the single aim of getting the results you want. One aim should be to have less mess, less stress and more success in your work.

Using Fear to Get Going

A new place or a new contact or strange conditions generate a kind of fear. There is hesitation before undertaking something new or unusual. Quite often, it can take great effort to overcome what frightens us. Our fears stop us in our tracks and keep us from peak performance. The best way to face any fear is to do something totally unrelated to it. A physical activity like getting up, walking around, jogging or some other diversion will help. The physical act of movement loosens the tension in our muscles so that we can control our emotions. If you put some time and space between yourself and the problem, it will reduce the magnitude of your problem. Doing something relieves tension. It is wise to use the adrenaline of fear for action, and not for suffering a feeling of being abandoned and/ or deserted. Only if you keep up such an attitude, can you start the intellectual process for handling the situation.

Fear is a normal and accepted part of life. It alerts us to potential problems. It also enhances our awareness of the opportunities which any situation presents.

Pay Your Taxes

Most intelligent people including some doctors, lawyers, top corporate personnel, even entrepreneurs do not have the vaguest idea of how to manage their finances. Throughout our lives, whether young or old, we must learn the obligation of paying taxes. And as soon as they have their own money, our children, too, must learn that when they spend money, they immediately become consumers. And all consumers of goods and services, no matter how young, must pay taxes. We are all part of a society. For the society to function appropriately, we need facilities like good roads, water supply and electricity. There are things we cannot do individually, neither do we want to, like building and maintaining a public street or a public park or a public walking place. Even if we wanted to, the cost and infrastructure required will be beyond our means. It would need too much time and money. So it is the government which has to do such things for us. It is the government which maintains the streets, the sidewalks, the police, and the fire department. All these have to be paid for, and for this reason we pay taxes to the government. It is our duty to pay our taxes for the common good. It does not mean that we pay more than we have to. By all means, we are entitled to take advantage of the incentives or deductions that are available. Take advantage of all legitimate deductions and pay your taxes happily to enable the government to provide citizens freedom, safety, security and justice. The 70/30 rule is an excellent one and it means that after you pay your share of taxes, you should learn to live on 70 per cent of your after-tax income. This is important. The 70 per cent income should be spent on both necessities and luxuries. Of the balance 30 per cent, one-third should be for charity, which is an act of giving back to the community what you have received in order to help those who need sustenance and funding. The rest of the 30 per cent should be used to try to create wealth. You can invest a part of this money on real estate or other commerce or manufacture. Use your imagination. You should make all purchases at wholesale rates. You can purchase a piece of property, improve it and then sell it at appropriate time. And if you are fortunate enough, you will make good money. If you work at a place where you earn rewards and incentives for additional productivity, you can increase your income through hard work, and use this to invest in an ownership position through the purchase of stocks of your company or other companies. You can also use the 30 per cent to purchase equipment, products, or gadgets like computers. You can work full time on your job and part time on making your fortune. You should aim to become wealthy and not just to pay your bills. Have a wealth plan to keep yourself motivated. The correct definition of "rich" and "poor" is that poor people spend their money and save what is left, and rich people save their money and spend what is left. You should also save some money and use the facility of compound interest. Make extensive use of tax-free retirement programmes. This way, you can accumulate a princely sum over the years.

Savings is the most exciting part of a wealth plan, as it offers you peace of mind by preparing you for the "winters" of life. The old philosophy was of spending money and saving what was left. The current philosophy should be of saving first and spending what is left. And this is what makes one man poor and the other wealthy.

Give, invest and save and it will show results, not in a day, or a week, or a month. But after five or ten years, the differences and the results will become pronounced and dramatic. It all starts with the same amount of money, but a divergent approach.

3
Motivate Your Employees

Right Way to Motivate Your Employees

Fear, incentives and growth are three most important methods to stimulate and prompt people in general. Let us examine their roles. Fear is neither suitable nor enjoyable, nor appropriate, and even not acceptable by most people. It also does not work systematically and clearly in the long-run. It is certainly not the best approach for the overall health of the organisation. However, there are people who use it and make blatant or veiled threats in order to get work done. Depending upon the kind of person you are dealing with, in some cases, it may be justifiable, when you want deadlines to be adhered to. The other way is to give incentives. John Maxwell says : "What gets rewarded, gets done." In other words, "If you do this, then you will get this." This approach works only for a while. It will yield results only for some time. For instance, the Government of India, gives the same percentage of bonus to one section of its employees, below the Group A, whether they work or not. After a time, most people come to treat the incentives as a matter of right. So this approach loses its effectiveness after some time. Every person has within him or her a desire to do better and excel. Some people are keener than others to fulfill this desire. But basically every person wants recognition for having done the job well. This is a great motivating factor. Personal growth and development need to be made the core values of an organisation. The management should provide regular opportunities for personal and professional growth to all its members. There are always opportunities and needs for professional growth, and each employee looks forward to it. Personal growth opportunities, with no strings attached, serve as the best incentives. Appreciation and rewards do bear fruit in due course of time.

Build Strong Relationships

Challenges on both personal and business fronts confront us every day. Each brings us new battles to be fought or won. This is irrespective of whether we want them or not and whether we are up to them or not. Life forces us to face one encounter after another. We have no choice in the matter. What we can choose, though, is to be either a victor or a victim. Being a victim assumes having bad relationships. Most people are victims. They are victims of their own way of thinking.

Most people are conditioned by their thoughts that tell them how to fight their battles, and what they can and cannot do. These tormenting thoughts have preconceived judgements about situations or persons. They can both encourage and discourage. Millions of people accept the judgments of their mental promptings as the truth. The consequence is mediocre results. With so many people living this way, the question arises: are people condemned to live this way all their lives. Fortunately, the answer is no, not unless you want to live that way.

Once you identify your mental inhibitors and how they hold you back, you can move beyond the role of victim and assume the role of victor. You can take command of the situation and positively influence your relationships, your options, in any aspect of your life. Take the following actions for building stronger relationships.

Show appreciation through your actions. You can say to someone, "I don't know if anybody else has told you this, but you speech was excellent. You have a wonderful ability to communicate your vision, that helps the rest of us in our roles and tasks. It is an excellent quality and is greatly appreciated." You can also show your appreciation through a card, a gift, or by spending some time with the person. Make it your goal to praise at least five people every day. If possible, praise ten people a day. Or perhaps you can try to praise everyone you come in contact with. It will make your day. The praise must be genuine for something done or attempted or for a quality, and it should not be phoney. There is a lot of power in praising people, both for them and for you. However, this requires a feeling of commitment to relationships. Such an emotion is supported by the conviction that the other person cares about you, that he values the association with you. If we believe that we are important to each other, important enough that we think of each other with warmth, most likely we will remain friends, even if we do not meet for a long time.

Psychologists say that if you act assertively most of the time, you are more likely to have satisfying relationships than if you act in non-assertive or non-aggressive ways. They suggest that you take the steps necessary to develop friendship. You can adopt the following networking techniques:

• *Always smile* – Have smile on your face. Be happy that you are alive wherever you are. Go out of your way to make the first move to cultivate people. Do not talk about yourself all the time when meeting others. Instead, ask questions about who they are and what they do.

• *Ask for business or visiting cards* – When you meet someone, and want to establish a relationship, ask for the person's business card. If he doesn't have one, write down his name and address on a piece of paper or on the back of your card. Your effort should be to collect the names and addresses of everybody who matters, whom you meet.

• *Add people to your mailing lists and contacts* – When you get back to your home or office, go through your collection of cards and add them to both your mailing list and your contacts. Categorise them carefully. Often we collect cards, but just stack them up, forgetting where we had met these people and in what context. You can make use of computers for categorisation and storage of such contacts lists.

• *Follow up with phone calls* – Schedule follow-up calls with the people you would like to know better or maintain regular contact with. When you contact them, do not give the impression that you are cultivating them for furthering your interests. Instead, let them feel that this will be a mutually beneficial and supportive relationship. Don't expect others to contact you, because they may not be as good at networking and keeping in touch.

• *Act as if it were your party and you were the host* – When you are at a networking occasion, do not miss an opportunity to meet new people. Act as if it is your party and you are the host, for better confidence. This will induce you to smile, be outgoing, and inspire you to meet other people.

Do Not Allow Your Desktop to Turn into a Catastrophic Quarter

Speaking from personal experience, most people, including myself, have a huge challenge coping with incoming paperwork. I fill up two waste paper baskets at the end of the day, despite my effort to make my home office a paperless office. In fact, since paper is my bread and butter, it lands on my desk and finds its way into the folders. Sometimes, it spreads out all over my study room, because pressure of work results in less important things or papers being kept pending. The result is a messy place.

The best course is to deal with the paperwork the moment it lands on your table. The other option is to let it pile up and then take your time to sort and deal with it, and tidy up the pile. This only means postponing the evil day. It is frustrating, when you need to search through a pile of papers to look for information. At the end of the search, you cannot locate it and find that it got mixed up with something else. An unattended pile of paper can cause you stress. Looking at it is enough to raise anyone's blood pressure.

To avoid the frustration and save yourself from such confusion, it is better to sort your papers and place them in folders marked Correspondence, Reading, Clients, Bills & Invoices and Staff Matters, etc. This is the only way to work in a manageable way. It's much more effective than dealing with shambles of paper. This approach can free you and your staff for other productive work, causing a saving of thousands of rupees. It's always the little things in life, which make the difference.

What a Boss Looks for in Subordinates

Many people want to ask their bosses why, despite their hard work, they are just plodding along in their jobs, not advancing as they had hoped to. How is it, that in the perception of people who work hard, their boss feels that some employees contribute so much, while others contribute so little? This question has remained both unasked and unanswered. With my four decades of experience, both as an employee and as a boss, I have discovered that most successful employees behave in similar ways and have common attitudes. If you want to move up, here are some principles I think you need to know: Do not behave like a kid, who keeps on running to the boss for everything. You should learn to take care of your work yourself. Do not always be a complainer and carry tales against others. It never pays. On the contrary, it gives the impression of your being a sissy and a backbiter. However, if you must go to the boss with a problem, take along a possible solution also. It will give the impression that you are capable of handling the problem and only want to make doubly certain that you will not fail. Everybody has problems. It is the steps you take for solving them that count. My suggestion is: when you face a problem, start looking for a possible solution. Problems should be treated as opportunities to showcase your talents and make a valuable contribution to your organisation's growth. Fix a problem before it becomes unmanageable.

You can create opportunities for further promotion by working beyond the defined limits of your job description. Nothing enthuses bosses more than employees who meet problems head-on. Nobody is perfect. Many people think that if others see a few imperfections in them, their chances of success will fade away. Such people remain in the background for fear that they will slip up and reveal that they are not perfect. The only way to avoid making mistakes is never to do anything innovative. Only that employee will make a mistake, who is willing to do something new and creative and is immersed in his job, and is not only thinking of the future. People who play safe and stay at home, do not reach an exotic destination.

Many people feel that they are entitled to a promotion or a job. Most employees believe that just doing their job passably and being available long enough, entitles them to raise. Just doing a good job is not sufficient to get promoted. Chiefs in any organisation expect everyone to work hard and do a good job, as they are paid for the same. It is more important to perform beyond expectation and let the boss know that you have the capacity to work well, both today and tomorrow in a higher position. From the boss' point of view, promotion is one of the methods to achieve the goals of the organisation. If the superiors believe that an employee cannot handle the new job, no amount of hard work, recommendations, lip service or sycophancy, can get you promoted, at least in the private sector. Things are different in the government, where everybody, after some years of service, feels entitled to a higher rank. In any case, the concept of the right to promotion is reinforced subterfuge. You have to sell yourself, and let your boss know about your accomplishments, talents, skills and potential. It is for the employee to bring his performance to the notice of the boss and sell himself as an excellent worker.

You have to talk in terms of the boss' language. You have to sell your talent, your capacity for more work and responsibility. You should also show your readiness for it. Certainly everybody wants more money. But the important thing is to ask for it in a way that emphasises that you are willing to work for it. By using this approach, you can work your way up to the top level, or start your own business and become a billionaire. Give yourself a chance to move up. Opportunity does not knock only once. In fact, it is knocking all the time. The problem is that often it knocks and we do not hear it. At every step and every turn of life, there is an opportunity. There is an opportunity in every job and in every offer that is made to us. Be willing to accept more work and responsibility, unless it is a technical job for which you do not have the qualification or you know you are not capable of doing it. The fact is that we can all grow into any work or job we do. Do not wait for the perfect environment or circumstances. Always be willing to handle a new job, if an offer comes your way. You should accept additional responsibilities without hesitation. You may feel that you cannot handle new responsibilities as you are already overloaded with work. These feelings are normal whenever new responsibilities are entrusted to people. But as long as you can swim, jump right in and paddle in the river of life. You can learn the finer points later. Develop the right contacts and friends. Contacts, associations and relationships are important in any organisation. Have a mix of friends, not only at your own level, but also at higher levels, who can help you understand the management's point of view. Cultivate friendships and develop relationships with positive people who think well of your organisation, the other employees and themselves. Avoid the moaners and fault-finders as they will try to dilute your optimism. Do not criticise your organisation in front of your colleagues and friends. This will come back to haunt you, as it is bound to be conveyed to your bosses, to your detriment. Never develop an attitude that puts the management on one side and the employee on the other. Both are part of the same organisation and one cannot survive without the other. It is not necessary to become a workaholic to reach the top. But as a matter of principle, never confine your work to a ten-to-six slot. When the boss has an important assignment to complete, he looks for people who are willing to get fully involved, without looking at the clock. He wants people who are eager to come to work in the morning and leave late, so that the goals can be accomplished.

Dealing with Criticism and Anger

When we find that things are not working out, as we want them to, we feel stressed and pushed. The two courses generally adopted are either to criticise those who apparently are the causes of the non-fulfillment of our desires, or to be arranged with those connected with the project. Basically, non-fulfillment of our expectations or hopes leads to our criticising others. Life presents us all kinds of situations. All are not exactly of our making or of our liking. God has made each human being different. Everybody has a different perception of each situation or event. There are more than one ways of doing the same thing. The question is, though we realise that criticism and anger are futile why do we still allow these deadly enemies to overpower us.

One way to deal with such situation is to write down our thoughts, about why we are critical and irritated. Quite often, after writing these down, we realise that we are making a mountain out of a molehill. Writing down your critical and angry thoughts is like an "undo" option on a computer. A situation of anger or criticism can be undone using this option. We can rid ourselves of the criticism, unreasonable anger and rudeness and our guilt if we sort things out clearly in our mind, by putting them on paper. Sometimes criticism is sought to be justified to drive home a point. But the fact is that in real life, those who are being criticised, focus on our emotions and not on the point we are trying to make. What we say in criticism draws more attention than why we are being critical. It is also a fact that the person against whom the criticism is directed, normally adopts a defensive and a self-righteous approach. In a rational state of mind, the person being criticised, would be inclined to accept a argument. But reasonable criticism, no matter how justified always causes resentment.

It is true that sometimes criticism is necessary to achieve results or reach a particular target. It should always be remembered that human beings can be quite irrational at times. Sometimes, even the most reasonable reason does not move them, more so, when it is a question of their self-respect and self-esteem. Any criticism has the effect of lowering the same. So an approach which yields the maximum dividends with the minimum of friction will yield best results. How do we adopt it?

There are a number of techniques by which we can control our instincts to be critical and angry. We must make an effort, to defuse the tendency to be critical. Slowly counting till ten, when you get angry and tend to be critical, is one of the best approaches. The logic behind it is that when we get angry, we lose our sense of proportion and rationality. We say critical words, without realising their gravity. Counting up to ten instantly shifts the focus, and hence the state of mind. It gives time for better sense to prevail. In this way, we can avoid doings things or expressing an opinion for which we may have to feel sorry later on.

Any delay in dealing with a problem can lead to missing the opportunity to limit the damage. Life gives us plenty of situations and options of losing our temper or staying calm or criticising or praising people. Hardening of attitudes makes most people justify their stand. People in such situations use sentences like, "Nothing wrong in my getting at what he said." It is a human tendency to underplay one's own role, though one might have started the tussle and the other person was merely retaliating.

Another technique of controlling your anger is that instead of shouting or yelling, take a piece of paper, and write down, whatever you want to say to the person you want to criticise. Do not edit or be polite. Write down exactly what comes to your mind, including abuses or foul or unparliamentary words. The very process of writing these down will vent your criticism and anger. It will also make you feel better. Address all the abuses you want to heap on that person. Preserve this paper, read it several times. This will enable you to let off steam, and you will realise the futility of criticism. It is the undo option. After some time, you yourself will destroy the paper. If you still feel the need for criticism and you feel it is justified, it can be conveyed with the same points, but politely, either verbally or through a letter. You can always convey your displeasure courteously. Practise this in writing. This will also enable you to do it in your speech. Some people use anger and criticism to get their demands conceded, like children bullying their parents and throwing tantrums. This approach might succeed with members of your family but not with outsiders, who would not be as tolerant, as parents.

Well channelled, that is, transmitted criticism and anger can generate tremendous energy, which can lead to tremendous achievement. This energy can be used in appropriate ways, instead of breaking household items or losing your temper on people. When you are really angry, you can well your temper by playing in a physically demanding game like tennis, badminton, squash, hockey, football or cricket. When you hit the ball, pretend that you are hitting the person you are angry with. Games and vigorous physical exercise will help you vent your anger harmlessly.

For example, if you are angry with someone and you are playing hockey or football, you can smash the ball and feel relieved without appearing foolish. Your angry vigorous game may even make your side win. But one definite effect it will have on you is to allow you defuse your anger and critical emotions. At the same time, you would have channelled your danger towards a positive achievement. For those artistically inclined, another way could be to write poetry or make a painting as a means to vent your anger. You can take your revenge in a gentlemanly way through those activities and still maintain your poise. You can make cartoons of the entire problem and make fun of the person through your cartoons, which can be laced with humour.

Sometimes, anger at the system and society leads people to become cynical. This leads to a negative view of everything. It is important to guard against becoming cynical. Instead, do something to rectify the system such as writing letters to newspapers about the problems which makes you critical. On several occasions, the inefficiency of the administration or injustice to the people provokes us to anger. One way of rationalising the anger is to do your best to attack the problem and the system, rather than the individuals, if the fault is that of the system and not of the individuals. However, if the fault lies with the individual, point out the lapse, rather than condemning the individual. It will motivate the individual to take interest in the work and make sure that such a lapse, leading to criticism, does not occur again.

The Gift of Self-Respect

Friends, colleagues and family are important. But nobody has the right to ruin your happiness, your marriage, or most importantly, your own and your children's self-esteem. You are a victim only as long as you allow or tolerate insulting or bad behaviour by others to continue against you. Ultimately, you have to draw the line somewhere and stand up for yourself. Only you can decide when enough is enough. Only you can decide that you will not allow yourself to be trodden upon.

You do not have to accept anybody's abusive behaviour, because of their position or your associations or relationships. None is entitled to mistreat you just because they happen to be in a dominating situation vis-à-vis yours. Otherwise, parents would have the right to abuse their children, men and women to abuse their spouses and bosses, their subordinates. In fact, it should be the other way around, where people more advantageously placed should be kind. Usually, people are afraid of bullies, afraid of what some person will do if he/she does not have his/her way all the time. It is a tough deal. But please keep in mind that you were not put on this earth to be anyone's emotional punching bag. The question arises: what are you going to do about a bully? Instead of dreading confronting such persons, figure out ahead of time how you are going to deal with him and still keep up your spirit intact. Instead of being able to accept happily, some people worry about the behaviour of others. Specifically, all the worry is about being verbally attacked, or being called names or taunted by others. A bully is usually a person trying to control and manipulate others. If by any chance you become a target you have the choice of either confronting the bully or allowing him to harass you. Sometimes, we are advised to ignore someone's bad behaviour, tolerate it, for the sake of good relations, or for the sake of the family name. It is advised that as long as the behaviour is not hurtful or malicious, then it can be ignored. It is also cited as justification that this person has been behaving equally badly with everybody. Well, I do not agree, as spiteful comments and other belittling behaviour is by the very definition, hurtful and malicious.

Our basic instinct is to retaliate when we are hurt or angry. This does not always succeed, as a bully is prepared to resort to sneaky, underhand tactics that a person with integrity wouldn't even dream of using. A bully is not above using deceit and manipulation to eliminate or discredit you if you expose him. A bully will pretend to be the victim in order to manipulate and control the situation. These tactics will make the bullied person more angry and isolated. The first step in dealing with a bully is to control your anger and not let the bully break your spirit. Channelise your anger into something positive in your life and do not sacrifice your integrity. It is hard to ignore someone like this, but it can be done if you deflect the spite with humour or repeat to the bully what he had said and then calmly declare, "I'm sorry you feel that way. But I am clear in my views." In other words, let the bully know that you are not going to allow him to humiliate you. Another technique is to tell him that he is acting gracelessly and say, "As far as I am concerned, the matter is closed. I don't want to discuss this issue any further." However, if you simply cannot bear being in the same room as your persecutor and he may not spare you, then spend as little time as possible in his company. Depending on your situation, you can either walk away or avoid any get-together where the bully may be present.

However, if somebody has bullied you in the past, recall how you handled that event and whether you could have handled it differently. How did it make you feel then and how would you now feel if such a bully was around? What can you do to transform your desire into a reality? Make a list of the ways in which someone is trying to manipulate you and devise possible solutions or responses to his behaviour. In short, ask yourself what would you do if you had to face such a person again. Write a letter, without any holds barred and put down in black and white, how to deal with the person who has been bullying you. Read this letter three times. But do not send it. It will release your pent up feelings.

You should focus on living a happy and successful life and on becoming the best person possible. Adversaries and bullies hate it when you excel, and rise higher than them with your integrity intact. Focus on your happiness and not the bully or the bully's concerns. A bully behaves the way he does because he feels inadequate or insecure in some way. The best long-term defence for dealing with a bully is to maintain and keep building your self esteem. You must not lose your right to be happy even if you have bullies in your life trying to show you down. The trick lies in getting through it without losing your temper or integrity and on focussing on the kind of person you want to be. Recognise and realise that bullies target you because you possess qualities that they envy and which make them feel inadequate in some way. Your goal should be to enjoy your life and not to let anyone ruin or disparage it.

Just Do It

Goethe said, "Whatever you can do, or dream you can, begin it. Boldness has genius, power and magic in it."

Many times we think that we cannot meet a new target or do something extraordinary. The best way to tackle this is to build a lasting confidence to do the things that surprises you at your own ability. Underconfident people do not set high standards for themselves. So they do not see themselves as achieving high standards. The result is that they do not consider it worthwhile to put in much effort. Give your ambition a go, whatever it might be. You have only this life to live and this is the only chance you have got. Do not avoid life and its problems. Do not make it boring and unexciting by not venturing in new directions, towards new goals.

To truly succeed in life, conscious understanding is generally not enough. We need to experience or devise a new skill or feeling, or delve into a new direction, to involve the unconscious with our goals. Involvement of the 'unconscious', is absolutely vital to building up of our self-confidence. Another way, which I have tried myself, is to build up self-confidence by using audio tapes of good and inspiring thoughts to encourage me. I listen to them during my morning walk, or during the time I necessarily have to spend in the bathroom. These tapes are recorded in my own voice and so there is no difficulty in absorbing what I have recorded. Incidentally, each one of us, spends a minimum of one to two hours in the bathroom. I have been listening to my tapes in the bathroom for more than two decades. Students can memorise or learn their subjects by putting the same on a tape and listening to it. I also use such confidence building tapes, interspersed with music, on my walkman, during my morning or evening walks. This means a great saving of time. By following this practice, I do not have to set aside time just for listening to the tapes. Listening is combined with walking, which is a mechanical activity.

Khushwant Singh, a well known columnist, wrote a piece on me, on this practice, which he felt was egoistic. I told him that I was not being egoistic, but realistic, gaining self-confidence in myself through a well-known method of hypnotism. The only difference was that I was hypnotising myself. This way, you can also hypnotise yourself, and develop the qualities you wish to cultivate. You can develop a feeling of trust in your own abilities. This method will allow you to feel comfortable in new situations and to see new opportunities in the old situations. This approach will keep you motivated. It will give you a quick dose of confidence boosting when you need it. Most importantly, it impacts directly on the emotional aspect of under confidence. It will also help you to re-pattern your unconscious mind in such a way that you can respond to situations in the way a confident person would. Use any method which suits you and gives you the results to helps you forge ahead in life.

The idea behind all these exercises is to feel good and to approach things with a carefree attitude, exploring the same, with the curiosity of a child, smilingly, confidently in the face of adversity, knowing that whatever happens, will happen for the best. Never forget that self-confidence is partly conscious, partly unconscious. It is all a question of thinking more confidently. Some may say that if you are feeling terrible, this will not help. But if your approach to life is positive and your unconscious is full of confidence building ideas, you will never feel terrible. It is important to go on practising powerful exercises for restructuring the way you think about difficult situations. You can always feel positive about a situation if your thinking is not a slave to your feelings. Negative thinking can erode good feelings over time. If there is a particular situation that you find difficult, use new responses to old situations. Develop a personalised exercise, or a method or a way of working that will leave you feeling refreshed and relaxed. This is the only way terrified people can become excellent public speakers. Just like poetry, an encouraging approach and language appeal more to the brain. This approach will also enable the listener to have a pleasant and happy experience.

Before starting anything, as a general approach, first take some time to get comfortable and have a few minutes for yourself. Like poetry, you need to absorb the words you are going to use, rather than examine them. Form a habit of reading slowly and deliberately to fully understand the significance of what you are reading or are going to do. Take time to explore the concepts you come across. This is part of our personality which encourages us to have faith in ourselves and trust our abilities to go forward to bigger achievements and responsibilities in our lives. Many surprising and quite often uplifting things happen beneath the surface, in our lives. Sometimes, such happenings make us feel good, The idea behind all these approaches is to develop an effortless ease, of gliding smoothly and freely on the highway of life, like an eagle, which is confident that it can fly high. Take time to increase your confidence in your own abilities, so that you can enjoy a life full of confidence and high self-esteem.

4
A Recipe for Success

Nine-Minute Organising Formula

You can achieve an incredible amount in just nine minutes. Here are a few ideas.

Nine-minute chore box

Rather than spending hours organising, and doing what you want to do all by yourself, list chores which can be done in nine minutes. Create a chore box for yourself and for each family member, if they are in a position to help you, in view of their age or qualifications. On a weekly basis an assignment should be clubbed and then divided according to what can be done by each tasks. This leads to more accomplishments and more output. To prevent any possible demoralisation or giving up of the scheme, make sure that each indicated task is completed in the assigned time.

You should make sure that the tasks are geared to, and in consonance with, a person's abilities (e.g. while adults do the heavier tasks, the youngsters may be assigned appropriate work). Each day, you should complete whatever you undertake. When all the assigned tasks have been completed and the box is empty, it can be refilled, and the system starts all over again. This system also works well at the office.

Nine-minute pick-up

Control the chaos, which if not prevented, can overtake us both in our houses and offices. Schedule a consistent, nine-minute tidying up each night. You can set a timer to sound the alarm in nine minutes. Make it a fun game for the entire family and when the alarm goes off, all family members should be involved in clearing out and keeping their belongings from the main family area. They should use this period to tidy up their work and living spaces. Applaud yourself and your family for what you have accomplished in nine minutes.

Most people postpone work on the pretext that they will do it "when they have time". This is one of the most common excuses used by a majority of people. The problem is that the time never seems to come due to numerous distractions. Nine minutes a day is the solution to "I'll do that when I have the time".

If you *really* want to accomplish something, you can generally find the time. For example, if you were to win an all-expenses paid trip to Europe and the trip was to take place by a particular date, you would find the time to fit it into your schedule, however busy you may be, without much of a problem. Similarly, you can begin fitting in the things you want to do, and can do in nine minutes, if you have a goal. Goals can help us in regulating our activities. You can schedule any nine minutes activity every day to catch up on your reading, or to do decluttering or have fun with your children. Then, work regularly on those nine-minute goals when the fixed time of the day rolls around. However, you should also schedule a few nine-minute luxuries per day to do something nice for yourself.

Sometimes, the day is so rushed and chaotic, that it's easy to forget the really important things like family, health, spirituality, personal time, and so on. Take your nine-minute vacation every day.

Hone Your Abilities

In today's fast-paced life and world, the victors are usually those with exceptional skills and abilities. The mediators are left behind. The race is always won by the one who has the skill. There are some ways to hone your abilities, and become successful and achieve greater aims in your life. Visualise the benefits of improving your abilities. Put them at the top of your mind and saturate your mind with the motivation. It will help you increase your abilities. For increasing your competence and abilities, you should be dissatisfied with your present state in life.

Growth for growth's sake, as well as for one's own sake is good. Those who achieve much are those who convince themselves that they want to grow and be better, and are willing to do whatever it takes to get there. They are not satisfied with their current state. It is this dissatisfaction, that will create in you a drive to achieve. The rewards that will accrue through your increased ability, and how you will be better off than others around you should act like an incentive and propel you forward.

Recognise your weaknesses

The best way to improve is to start with areas in which you are particularly inadequate. Depending upon how much interest you take, it is easy to improve at something you are not good at rather than something you already do well. Take some time to assess the areas you are weakest in. Then focus on them for a while. The results will be much more pleasing and pronounced than getting enhanced at something you are already good at. And in things you are already good, aim to reach even greater heights. Stretch yourself to the limit in an area, in which you already have some skill and ability.

Which areas you want to excel in is for you to decide. When you leave your weaker areas, and make extraordinary gains in your one strong area, then you will be moving forward. That is the only right course, which should fit in with your overall goals. Allocate time each day to self-improvement. This is the only way to steady advancement in life. In fact, you may not discern any improvement for days or weeks. You may feel that despite your efforts, you are not succeeding. But with persistent efforts, you will eventually get to what you want. This will increase both your skill and competence. The secret is to spend all your time in bringing about improvements. Spending just ten minutes a day equals roughly to one hour a week, two hours a month and one full day in a year. Remember to practise repeatedly. Identify people who have greater competency than you. For increasing your ability, meet, observe, study and interact with them, if possible. This interaction or even competition with people more skilled than you will make you better. It is exactly like in games and sports, wherein to improve your performance, you play with players better than yourself. Decide on a specific skill or ability you would like to improve upon. Recognise and spot someone who is a specialist in the area and study how he has reached the top. You can also buy audio or video tapes to help you grow in your selected areas. These tapes are available in the market. You can also make your own tapes. Be slow but sure, be the proverbial tortoise, not the hare. Share something of yourself and your good qualities with others. Be spontaneous with others. It will make you not only popular, but win you many friends in high places.

If you are happy and fulfilled, you will be glad to build up others who need such help. It is a boon, to invest in the lives of others by praising and encouraging them. Even if you never get anything in return, it is the right thing to do. By building up others, you also create a good impression about yourself. An unthinking and inconsiderate person denigrates others. But successful person will instil in them the power of success through praise. Take time to do things right and keep on going in the right direction. Learn your job correctly, in a professional way. Never give up excellence for speed. The whole idea of acceleration is to have a slow start, work up to a high speed, and then go the whole hog. Fortunately, life is not a hundred-metre dash. It is a marathon, where the ultimate arrival at the final destination, however slowly, matters. Life is what you make of it and it is happiness in life which matters the most. Happiness is essentially is a state of going somewhere, whole-heartedly, uni-directionally, without regret or reservation. Never be afraid to take a big step if one is required. You cannot cross a big, deep hole or a large gap in two jumps.

Have a Stress-Free Life

Well off people have clothes and shoes littered all over the place. Such a clutter is not welcome. Instead get yourself a two or three shoe racks and organise your shoes in one place. Put your fancier shoes on one shelf, and your casual shoes on another. The third tier can be for shoes you use at home. Our homes are littered with all kinds of paper – paper which has outlived its utility and is fit only for the dustbin. If you have not looked at or seen any file for years together, unless it is of property or bank matters, the chances are that you are not going to look at it for another few years, or till such time the papers are no longer needed. Take out the thickest file folder in your filing cabinet and weed out anything outdated.

Get a new calendar every year and mark on it for all recurring events such as birthdays, anniversaries, and so on. Also, fill in any other events and appointments you've already scheduled. Use highlighters and markers. Highlight your calendar so that you can see at a glance what is coming up. For instance, highlight all birthdays and anniversaries in blue, all appointments in green, and all project dates in yellow. There is no fixed formula for any colour scheme. You can choose any colour scheme. Working will be easier if you organise yourself regularly. Make a list of five people you have been wanting to call. Write down their numbers and then plan the time for talking to them. Keep all clippings from magazines for reference in one file. Read one book every month, and share what you read with a family member or friend. You do not have to buy a book every month. You should make it a habit to visit your local library, and become a member. Many people have clutter in their homes or place of work because they wait to arrange things, or delay throwing out something they no longer need. Things are put away temporarily, like on the dining table or desk, "just for now". The temporary storage areas often become clutter spots. For instance, if there is already one newspaper on your desk, you may reason, that it will not really make a big difference if three more newspapers are also kept there. The truth is it will make a huge difference. Before you realise it, you'll have an enormous stack of paper on your desk and you will have made your desk literally unworkable. We have a tendency to toss our jackets or socks or towels over the back of the sofa or a chair in the house. We may feel that it is only one item. Well, what if all the members of the family walk in and toss their items next to yours on the sofa or chairs? They have as much right to do what you do. If something is good enough for mother and father, they will argue, it is good enough for them too. It will not take long for your house to become a mess. If we ignore the small mess, it will soon turn into a bigger one. So the next time you consider tossing the mail on the dining table instead of going through it right then, or letting the laundry pile up all week rather than washing one machine load a day, remember that it will become an uncontrollable clutter. Most clutter can be avoided by simply taking a few minutes to put things away or getting rid of things you no longer need immediately. Every big problem was at one time a small problem that became a big nuisance later on. Clutter creates stress. You can avoid such stress in the following ways.

Keep a diary

Keep a list of things, events, times, places and people that seem to make you feel stressed out. Do it for at least a fortnight, preferably for one month, to get a clear idea. You will be astonished to find that a pattern soon emerges from this diary so as to settle the demands on you for doing too many things at once. Keeping a stress diary will help you to handle stress. It will help you find the stress levels you can tolerate better, the level where you can effectively operate under pressure. At that comfort level, you will understand the things that cause you stress. You can also assess how effective your stress control strategies are. Once you have maintained a stress diary for a number of weeks, you will be in a position to analyse it and develop an action plan to control the stress. Once you have identified your pressure points, you can consider adopting the following solutions. Treat your diary, like a good friend or your partner and put your thoughts in it, as if you are discussing things. Discussing things often makes you feel better. You will get the same feeling after reading your thoughts, if the same have been faithfully and impartially recorded. Your diary will give you advice to deal with the stressful situations that you have identified.

Plan breaks in your working day

The aim here is to allow time for unexpected events which always crop up during our lives every day. Getting up 30 minutes earlier than you usually do, will help you to get ready without rushing. Better still would be to get things ready the night before. Try to have 30 minutes in the morning or the afternoon as your exclusive time. This is the time in which you can do whatever you want, even if it is simply relaxing still and doing nothing. Look forward to these times when things get busy. Avoid smoking and alcohol, if you are using these as crutches. They do not help you cope. In the long-run, they make stress worse. Drinking to "calm your nerves" is no solution and is a slippery approach.

Strive for Success

There are different types of people in the world. Some work hard, and incessantly, to make things happen. Some are mere spectators who watch things happen. And there are some who analyse and who wonder why things have happened. It is for you to decide what kind of person you want to be. Success does not come our way merely through wishing for it. Neither can it be faced to fall into our laps. Trying to force success to happen, can lead to incredible frustration when things do not go according to our plans. More often than not you have to work like a dog to attain success. There is a price tag on success in any field of life. If you want to be extraordinary, you must undertake to do the things that ordinary people are not willing to do. All events in our life occur due to a reason. Every episode has a cause as you will see if you carefully attempt to understand why incidents happen the way they do. Sometimes, when things are beyond your control, it is necessary to "let go" or as has been said, "let go and let God handle it". But letting go and letting God handle it should not mean that you sit back and just pray for outcome, and do nothing about it. On the contrary, you are accountable for what is going to come to pass in your life. Achieving success in your life means organising all of the attributes for success

A Recipe for Success

in a manner that will produce your desired results not the outcome someone else feels you deserve. What are the factors which can lead to success? Depending on the outcome you want, you will have to fashion your own approach, based on the results you want. There are, however, some fundamental components, like passion, integrity, determination, focus, optimism, faith, a positive attitude, awareness, decisiveness, commitment and love, without which success is not possible. There is no single coaching programme that will uniformly produce the same results for all human beings, as all are unique. For bringing out the best in any human being, even in yourself, you need to understand individuals.

What brings out the best in a man is an understanding of his individuality. Make a thorough study to really understand yourself: your behaviour, your habits, your areas of focus, your daily rituals, your choices and your unique talents. Become acutely aware of what you are doing in your life. Keep on experimenting and discovering the methods of turning your talents into strengths that will in turn transform your goals into concrete achievements. If you want to be successful, find a role model, someone who is already successful in the line you are interested in. Observe the method they have used to succeed. If you cannot get access to them, read their writings or their interviews. Success is infectious and it breeds success in turn. Following another person's success technique or patterns will significantly reduce the time you will take to reach your goals. You will save time avoiding the mistakes that others have made. Your role "models" have gone through the obstacle race and reached their goals the hard way, after having learnt their lessons through trial and error. The successful people or role models have learned what to do and, more significantly, what not to do. It is best to follow their good points, and adapt the same to your conditions. If you must copy them, do it wisely. You can enhance your own success by fine-tuning and adjusting the success techniques of others to suit your goals. There is scope for continuous improvement in any method. Human beings are far more capable than they know or understand themselves. We all have unlimited potential. Men have done the impossible. The only thing that postpones our progress is our restrictive beliefs about our own abilities. If we believe we will not be able to do something, then we can never do it. Instead, we should adopt the philosophy of "there is a way " and "I will find it, and succeed in my mission". This approach makes the impossible possible. We have the ability to do anything we want with our life. We should be clear about our dreams, and trust ourselves, so that we are committed to our goals and don't let anyone or anything stand in our way or take our dreams away from us.

The Successful Person's Secret Weapon

The most important weapon in the armoury of a successful person is trust. The only way to build trust is to keep your word. If you make a promise, then keep it at all costs. Regrettably, most people do not deliver on their promises. Such people do not realise that the 'trust' element and their credibility goes down the drain and brands them as unreliable and untrustworthy people. People avoid transacting any business with these who are not worthy of trust and credibility. Even an ordinary person would not like to deal with someone he did not feel confident about. It is legitimate to ask the question: why do people overpromise and underdeliver, despite their best intentions? One reason is that most people rely on their memories and make promises verbally but do not write down the details of the work to be done for follow-up. It is not humanly possible to remember every single detail of the work to be done, every day. However, you are less likely to forget something if you keep a systematic record of the things to be done. Thousands of thoughts run through our mind each day, leaving the brain overcrowded. You can devise a system that suits your needs. But without a system, there is no way you can remember all you promise and wish to deliver. This is the only way to effectively plan your time, your activities, keep appointments and make sure you do as you promised. It is absolutely essential to have the reputation of a person who is trustworthy, reliable and credible. Make a checklist of everything you'd like to do for the day, as well as later on. Take control of yourself and invest time and money on yourself for your advancement and development. This is essential so that at some later stage in your life, you do not have to dance to someone else's tune and leave your future in someone else's hands. Unfortunately, most people drift along in life, accepting whatever is dished out to them. These are the people who do not bother about investing extra time, money or energy on themselves. Hence, the vast majority of people find it much easier to swim along with the crowd. Take stock, and ask yourself whether you have achieved the goals you set for yourself for the year. Have you been successful in making positive changes in the areas of relationships, finance, career, health, general fitness and well-being, etc. Ask yourself whether you are better off this year than the last year and whether you have moved forward or backward in life. Also ask yourself whether you are happy. The answers to these questions lie in whether you are only going through the motions of living or are excited about life, your achievements or your future. Finally, if you want to be a leader rather than a follower, you need to take action, and that too, from this very moment onwards. If you don't know where to go you cannot get anywhere. Do not waste time. Get moving today to have a great life and a glorious future. Good ideas and good intentions are worthless, if you don't take action. It is only action which generates momentum. With momentum you can achieve magnificent things. Even if it is taking just one step, go ahead to make a beginning for glorious results. This is the only way to get on to the fast track to success, as well as get motivated and focussed to increase your competence and market value. This approach will help in creating order out of chaos and create a happier and healthier workplace. It will also help you to organise your day, as well as your life, and increase your productivity. If you follow some of the above suggestions, you will develop a no-nonsense approach, which is just what everyone needs in one's job or profession.

Clothes Make the Man

Clothes are an important part of one's personality. If you are dressed like a gentleman, you act like a gentleman. Clothes give us an image to live up to. So dress well, don't dress like a bum.

Shakespeare said, "Apparel oft proclaims the man." He has highlighted the importance of dressing well, appropriate to the part one is required to play in life. We do not choose our roles in life. Our duty is confined to performing them well. Different occasions in life require different types of dress. Formal occasions require formal dress. You have to visualise the occasion, the type of people you would be meeting, the kind of effect your clothes would or should produce on them. Sometimes, comfort and convenience are to be sacrificed keeping in view the solemnity of the occasion. Even in hot weather, one has to wear a suit sometimes, as the occasion or host demands it. But these days, modern dress designers have also taken care of comfort, convenience, and the impression the clothes will most likely make. Your effort should be to not only look good, but also aim for the maximum impact through your dress and personality. Being well-dressed helps in confidence building. Being smartly turned out will single you out as a distinguished person. But no amount of dressing well can conceal a sloppy personality or posture. Do not go in for a style of dressing just because it is the done thing, or in fashion. Remember that how you wear your clothes is more important than what you wear.

Once I invited a doctor friend for dinner in Bangalore in 1976. He turned up with his grown up son who was wearing old, torn jeans. I was seething with anger to see such a slovenly dressed person in my drawing room. When I pointed it out to my wife after dinner, she told me that it was the latest fashion, known as bleeding jeans. I was considered old fashioned by the youth who pitied me for my ignorance. Notwithstanding the views of others, I am of the firm opinion that one should look one's best and be presentable at all times. We have to remember that our contact with other people, in business or meetings or our workplace, is limited. The first impression is created by clothes. It is always best to look your best. The idea of dressing well varies from place to place. In north India, a person dressed in dhoti and kurta is considered to be a rustic or backward person. The man wearing a suit is considered to be smart. In the south, dhoti and kurta is the traditional dress of the common man. Even Prime Ministers Deve Gowda and Narsimha Rao wear dhoti, kurta and pyjamas in Delhi.

In June 1963, I was going to my home town Jalalabad in Punjab from Mysore where I was under training as an Assistant Superintendent of Police. The metre-gauge train brought me to Bangalore from Mysore. The train had arrived late. I was in a hurry, to catch the connecting train to Madras, (present Chennai). I could not find a coolie quickly. I saw a person in dhoti and kurta boarding my compartment. Mistaking him to be an unlicensed coolie, I said, "Please pick up my luggage and take it to Madras Mail, which is on the other platform." He was surprised, and said, "Sir, I myself am a first class passenger." His politeness was a lesson in courtesy. In his place I would probably have been abusive and self-righteous. It taught me a lesson which I have tried not to forget: one must never judge any man on the basis of the clothes he is wearing.

Always be yourself, whether it is your conduct, or your dress. Never fall into the trap, of dressing merely for pleasing others. Dress only to highlight your personality and to show your better side. It is not only the fine feathers which make fine birds. It is the inbuilt strength of the birds themselves which takes them to great heights. Wear your clothes wisely and well. Dressing well should be a pleasure and its aim should be to heighten your personality and to impress. It is rightly said that a fool may have his coat embroidered with gold, but it is still a fool's coat. Good clothes cannot conceal basic flaws in character. Follow the Golden Rule, "Do unto others, what you would wish them to do unto you." It is an eternal law which clearly enunciates that we reap what we sow. If you deal unjustly with others, remember that unjust dealings will boomerang. Your acts of injustice and unkindness will return to you. You should not only ensure that your neighbour does not cheat you. But also that you do not cheat your neighbour.

It is important to add love to any human relationship and enjoy what you are doing. Do not be bound to do the work you do not like. Develop a habit of liking what you are required to do. Consider your potential and develop the habit of thinking big, with long-term objectives in view. Do not be tempted by short cuts and short-term rewards, at the cost of big achievements. Remember that a job done well has a future. All jobs have the potential to take you to the top. Liking what you do will keep you healthy. Do your best, and you will sleep soundly. Stress is the natural consequence of any task if you do not enjoy doing it. The key to happiness is doing your work joyfully. It will lead to happiness, success, and prosperity. There is no success without sacrifice, hard work, and dedication. According to A P Gouthey, "To get profit without risk, experience without danger, and reward without work is as impossible as it is to live without being born."

Simple Organising Ideas

Here are just a few, simple ideas that can help you get better organised.

• *Determine your goals* – Before you start anything, determine its goal. If you don't know where you're going, how will you ever get there? Set mini-goals and reward yourself for successes.

• *Declutter your desk* – An uncluttered desktop removes unnecessary distractions and helps keep your mind on tasks that need immediate attention. Keep only these items on your desk that relate to your current projects.

• *Don't rely on your memory* – You run the risk of letting tasks fall through the cracks. The best way to never forget an appointment, a deadline or a detail again is to write it down.

• *Consolidate similar activities* – Instead of starting and stopping at different levels of activity, you'll save time by making all of your outgoing telephone calls together, taking care of all your errands in one go.

• *Clean out your files* – Before you go through the expense of purchasing more file cabinets, folders, etc, take the time to discard all unnecessary paperwork and material.

• *Use one calendar* – The biggest mistake people make when using planning calendars is to keep more than one. Write personal, professional and family items on one calendar. It will help to eliminate scheduling conflicts. Remember, "the man who wears two watches, never knows the correct time".

• *Reduce telephone time* – Plan telephone calls (whether to doctors, plumbers, clients, etc) whenever possible. Have all

the necessary material in front of you. Write down key questions in advance.
- *Set up files for projects*
Don't waste time searching for papers when you need them. Keep all paperwork that pertains to a certain project together in one large folder.
- *Set time limits* – Say, "I've got only five minutes to talk." Outline your calls. Say, "I'd like to discuss these two possible solutions to the problem: A ..."
- *Make time for yourself* – Make at least one screened appointment with yourself each day. Screened time is quiet, uninterrupted time allowing you to concentrate on a project or catch up on your reading.
- *Delegate* – Realise that you can't do everything. Delegate work in the office and at home. To use an effective delegation system, you must train, trust, follow-up and evaluate.
- *Don't overstuff filing cabinets* – There's nothing worse than having to file papers in a file cabinet that is overloaded! Leave enough room in file drawers so that you're not using all your energy to get a piece of paper in or out.
- *Develop false deadlines* – If you have a deadline at the end of the month, record the deadline four days earlier. You'll eliminate the last-minute rush to complete the project because you'll have given yourself ample padding.
- *Use timers and alarm clocks* – Allocate time for your daily activities, from working on projects to doing household chores. Then set timers or alarm clocks to keep you on schedule.
- *Make good use of space* – Add shelves for reference books and manuals. Add space extenders in desk drawers. Buy full-suspension file cabinets. Use stacking bins.
- *Make the most of spare time* – Catch up on your reading while you wait for appointments. Audio cassettes of an educational or motivational nature are a great way to make use of your time while driving to work.

- *Get the kids off to school quicker* – The trick is not to leave decision-making for the morning. The night before help your children choose their outfits, decide what they want to eat and determine what they need for school.
- *Set time limits* – If you have to work late or during the weekend, set time limits for yourself. Whether you work for two hours or four, stop working at the end of that time and enjoy the rest of the evening or weekend.
- *Label things* – Don't just toss your spare keys in a shoebox without first identifying them. Label each item or packet.
- *Eliminate brushfires* – Brushfires are almost always caused by disorganisation. Eliminate the disorganisation and you'll eliminate the brushfires.
- *Determine your best time for tasks* – Use your most productive time to do your most productive work. Alert in the morning? Afternoon? Tackle your most difficult, important work during that time of day when you're at your best and you're most likely to complete it.
- *Use master lists and 'to do' lists* – Take control of your time. When used properly, these effective tools give you a specific idea of what you need to accomplish.
- *Set deadlines* – Setting a deadline forces you to work towards it. Set a definite date and time. Saying, "When I get a chance" or "Sometime in the near future" is insufficient.
- *Use a greeting card organiser* – Consider a greeting card organiser to remember birthdays, anniversaries and other special events. These look like notebooks except that each page has a monthly pocket to hold cards. You can pencil in birthdays, events, etc for each month, plus, you can purchase your cards ahead of time!
- *Plan your garden early* – Start planning your garden in the winter. Decide what you'll plant. Read up on the proper care of your plants, flowers and vegetables. Sketch your garden out on paper. When spring arrives you'll be ready to "grow".

- *Store similar items together* – Categorisation is very important when you are getting organised. Keep all bill paying supplies in one place. Gather all of your craft supplies in a basket. Keep your photo supplies in one plastic bin. When you need to work on something, everything will be easily accessible.
- *Categorise your files* – First, decide on broad categories according to the particular work materials in your office. Then, file alphabetically or chronologically within these categories.
- *Plan your meals* – Plan your meals before you write out your shopping list. It will save time because you'll know exactly what you need. Your meals should:
    (a) be well-balanced and nutritious;
    (b) offer variety;
    (c) be within your food budget;
    (d) fit your time and energy limit.
- *Put things away each day* – Take time to put things back where they belong. Put things back immediately after you're finished with them or set up a 15-minute appointment with yourself to put things back at the end of each day.
- *Toss out old reading material* – Go through your reading stack. Get rid of outdated newspapers. Ditch magazines older than three months. Keep only a few catalogues that you truly enjoy.
- *Clean out your library* – Look through your bookcases and give away books you've had for years and will never look at again. Charities are always looking for donations to their reading programmes.
- *Enlist your friends* – Does your house need to be painted? A great way to get the job done quickly is to throw a painting party. They supply the help. You supply the pizzas, sandwiches, beverages and dessert.
- *Keep receipts together* – Keep an envelope in your purse or wallet to hold receipts that you may need for expense records

or tax purposes. When you get back to the office, put the receipts in pre-designated envelopes (business meals, fuel, rental expenses and so on), then keep all the envelopes in a larger expanding file or box.

• *Ditch outdated computer stuff* – Toss out software disks, CDs, computer manuals, etc for computer programmes you no longer use and never will again.

• *Coordinate with others* – Work together with others—family, or co-workers—to come up with organisational systems that are simple and effective for everyone involved.

• *Use a desk organiser* – Keep a sufficient supply of pens, pencils, paperclips scissors and other necessary supplies in a desktop holder on your desk or a tray inside your desk.

• *Create an effective work area* – Create a pleasant, well-equipped work area. Whether it's a nook, cranny or a large office, your work area should be conducive to performing your daily work. It should contain all necessary supplies and equipment in easily accessible areas.

• *Magnetise your medicine cabinet* – Mount a long magnet along the back of your medicine cabinet to hold tweezers, clippers, little scissors and other small metal objects.

• *Rest and relax* – Get a good night's sleep (seven hours or more). Adequate rest at night will help you to be alert, on schedule and effective the next day.

• *Make your move easy* – Colour code your boxes with a self-stick yellow dot for those that go to the kitchen, red dots for the office, blue dots for the garage, and so on. Before you move into a new house, place the corresponding coloured dots in the appropriate rooms.

• *Prepare outgoing mail ahead of time* – If you are in a profession where you have to send the same brochures and other materials to prospective clients, make your packages ahead of time. Include all necessary materials and store them

away until you need them. They'll be all ready to go in a jiffy.
• *Create reference lists* – Reference lists are wonderful tools for remembering and accessing everything easily. Create reference lists for:
- Personal goals and dreams.
- Birthdays.
- Favourite restaurant phone numbers.
- Websites you'd like to explore.
- Books you'd like to read.
- Things to pack when travelling.
- Gift ideas for friends and family.
- Computer files.
- A wish list for yourself.
- ... and more. Your choices are endless!

• *Create forms for everyday tasks* – For example, type up your own Fax Transmittal Form that includes your name, company name and other pertinent information. Make copies and leave them by your fax machine for efficient and effective communication.

• *Create a driving directions folder* – Create a file folder for driving directions to places you go to infrequently. Write down the directions and keep them in this folder for future use. You won't have to keep asking for directions.

• *Give driving directions with ease* – Create driving directions to your home or office, coming from north, south, east and west. Make copies and keep in a file. When someone asks, you can mail them, fax them or read them over the phone.

• *Determine how long it will take* – Estimate how long it's going to take to get there. Divide the total miles of the trip, by your average speed (e.g. 60 mph). The result will be your driving time. (Example: 120 miles to be travelled divided by 60 mph is approximately 2.0 hours of driving time).

- *Cut down on junk mail* – Visit the Direct Marketing Association Website and ask them to remove you from direct mail lists you don't wish to be on: http://www.the-dma.org/consumers/offmailinglist.html
- *Combine your task* – Look for things you can combine to save time and accomplish more. Walk with your dog and you'll be exercising at the same time. Go to the beach with a motivational tape, and you'll be relaxing and getting inspired simultaneously.
- *End each day on a good note* – Save your easiest tasks for the end of each day. You'll be able to complete them, and end each day on a positive, rewarding note.
- *Improve continuously* – Get organised and stay organised.

Adopt Techniques for Faster Learning

The human brain has a capacity to store up to 280 quintillion (280,000,000,000,000,000,000) bits of memory. Everybody has the potential to be a budding genius like Sir CV Raman, Einstein or any other brilliant achiever. We all actually use only a fraction of our intelligence. But a stimulating, enriched environment can make a difference to your achievement level. Some tips which can facilitate are as under.

Read about subjects that require deliberation

These could be biographies, books on excelling in life, news magazines and newspapers. Read a non-fiction book for at least 15 minutes each day. Always carry reading material with you so that you can read the same, even if you have only few minutes. I always carry some reading material in my car. This way I have turned bits of idle time into learning time. Get an excellent dictionary and master the meaning of five new words a day. In one year, you will have mastered 1800 words and in ten years, it would be 18000 words, more than any ordinary human being knows at present. The dilemma with many people is that after they get past the age at which they should have learned something, they become embarrassed if they have not. They back away from anything and everything. They feel that they've been left too far behind and that catching up is too big a task.

Stop or reduce TV watching time

Watching television has become a habit for most of us. Most people, especially of the younger generation have grown up with it. But if you are serious about wanting to think better, and especially if you want to lengthen and strengthen your attention span, you need to control your TV watching time. If you must, then get the TV guide, look through it like a menu and form a conscious decision about the TV programmes, you want to watch. Do not waste your time on junk programmes as they are as bad for your mind, as potato chips are for your body. Set a personal development goal of gaining knowledge, in a specific field, on a particular topic. Convince your friends and family so that they can support you.

Be creative

We all have creativity inside us. Look at children. They can sing, mimic, dance, play musical instruments and paint wonderful pictures. Adopt the attitude that learning is a life-long process. Use it or lose it. Whatever be your age, you can always discover, something for, and about, yourself. Ask questions and take nothing at face value. Do not be a passenger in life, be an active participant in its journey. Do not merely follow somebody else's directions, though they may be excellent, unless you can adopt or suit them to your circumstances, and you feel that they constitute the best possible course in the circumstance. Remember that final responsibility for your actions is only your own. You have to fight your battles yourself, and on your own steam. When someone discusses something unfamiliar with you, and you do not understand it fully, ask him or her to explain it. The only silly question is the one you do not ask and remain ignorant.

Visualise

A powerful way to solve a problem is to use visualisation. Even if you think that you cannot visualise well, you will still get grand results with this approach. Write down your problem as precisely as you can. It is essential to be clear about the problem before you can solve it and get the best results. Bacon said, "Writing makes an exact man." Research has shown that geniuses and all who have excelled and made a mark in history were compulsive scribblers. Some of these geniuses were Sir Isaac Newton, Thomas Jefferson and Johan Sebastian Bach. They all documented their thoughts and feelings in diaries, poems, and letters to their friends and relatives. Researchers have noted this propensity not only in budding writers but also in generals, statesmen, scientists, and all others who have excelled in any sphere of life. Noting down and thinking about things will expand your mental power, make your intellect stronger. It will be of immense help in developing and using logic, which is of tremendous help in life. Like language, logic is basic to good communication. If you do not know what you are going to solve, you will naturally get no results. You can use coloured pens, and little symbols to get your thinking clear on all aspects of the problem you want to tackle. If you like, write down the problem in red ink, the possible methods for solving it in yellow, and the best method for solving it in green. Sit back, close your eyes and relax. It will be better if you let the problem simmer and wait for some time for the best solution to come to your mind.

Imagine yourself going down some steps, deep, deeper underground. You should feel more relaxed with each step downwards. Pass through an imaginary gate to a long, dimly lit tunnel. Go further down in your imagination and take your time over this. Imagine that there is a door inside, where there will be a clue and an answer to your problem. Remember what you see later, the ideas occur to you and the associations they bring up from within you. Accept what you see/feel/hear and do not be judgemental at this stage. Imagine yourself going back from the door and the tunnel. At the end of this process, write down exactly what you experienced, in as much detail as possible.

Analyse what you saw or felt in relation to your difficulties. What did you figure out? What solution did you get? What do you think you should be doing now? The best solution has most likely emerged out of this exercise. Keep a pen and notepad next to your bed so you can write down the answers you get the next morning. If you find it too cumbersome, and you can afford it, keep a dictaphone next to you for recording your ideas. You could be pleasantly surprised at the answers you get.

Work More Than You are Paid for

A sense of timing includes planning your best work, at the peak of your energy. For serious work, for answering important mail, you could allocate early time of the morning. You could set apart time for phone calls. Telephones have a way of disturbing you when you are doing your most serious work. You must set aside time for this. When your activity levels are low, use that time for telephone calls. Fixing a set time for meetings will enable you to plan for the rest of the day in a more productive way. Condition yourself for focussing your energy, concentration, and zeal for the tasks at hand. You can begin by accomplishing small tasks first.

A Recipe for Success

Reward yourself at every opportunity for any accomplishment, however small. Whatever task you undertake, set out to complete it. The sense of achievement and accomplishment will give the much needed energy to complete more difficult tasks.

As a person dedicated to achieve success, you should have an upright bearing and an impressive posture. You should appear to be full of energy. Your body should convey a sense of energy, with your head up and your stomach pulled in. You should give an impression of being a person who is full of life and alertness. We cannot convince people of our self worth if we appear lethargic, listless, and slow. Most people judge others by appearance.

A leader should seem dynamic, as if his vitality and energy, are barely held back. A successful person is normally careful about his diet. He cannot afford to stuff himself at the beginning of the day, starting off on a note of discomfort. He tries to make eating an enjoyable experience. So he selects his food carefully. His criteria for food is whether it will fatten him, or whether it will give him adequate energy, for the work at hand. I have noticed that whenever I have eaten a heavy breakfast or overstuffed myself, I am not fit for any quality work. This continues till the food has been digested and the stomach feels comfortable. So I try not to overstuff myself, however tempting the food may be. A successful person does not fight his natural inclinations and habits. For instance, if you do not like to have lunch, then make dates only for the meals which suit you. If you do not drink, do not go to parties where drinks are served, but stick to your own routine. If a successful person starts fighting his own inclinations and habits, he will have less or no energy, for the work at hand. A successful person respects and adjusts to his own inclinations and body needs for the best results. For instance, I try to avoid attending dinners as they take up a lot of time and interfere with my routine. Unless it is totally unavoidable, I invite people only for lunch and if invited, I convey my preference for a luncheon meeting.

A successful person has a built-in sense of responsibility and integrity. He can be counted upon to behave consistently and reliably, in almost all situations. He often asks himself the question: "What is the worst which can happen?" He tries to improve upon the worst, if he has to face it. A successful person devises his own ways of dealing with problems. He does not hesitate to talk to himself and take stock of situations by weighing their pros and cons. He sets deadlines to complete the task at hand. He realises that any open-ended course, without fixing time limit for the solution of the problem at hand will only deplete his energy and ability.

Machiavelli wrote in the 16th century, "This is to be asserted, in general of men, that they are ungrateful, fickle, false, cowardly, covetous, and as long as you succeed, they will offer you, their blood, property, life and children when the need is far distant; but when it approaches, they turn against you ... And men have less scruple in offending one who is beloved than one who is feared, for love is preserved by the link of obligation which, owing to the baseness of men, is broken at every opportunity for their advantage; but fear preserves you, by the dread of punishment which never fails ... " A few of the Machiavellian characteristics are essential to success in life. It is essential to recognise that simply giving of instructions to act in a particular way is no guarantee that the task would be done. A successful person builds in an element of supervision to get done what he wants done. A successful person is never shy of his own success. It is the best proof that he has nothing to be shy of or hide. He is always confident of his own values.

5
Feel Terrific about Yourself

Value Yourself

You are your most precious resource, your most valuable asset for achieving anything in life. It is important to keep feeling great about yourself all day long and all the time. The following suggestion can help.

Watch your weight

The first step is to be careful about your weight. Roughly one kg an inch is ideal for men and 0.80 kg for women. Having extra weight on your body is like always carrying a potato sack on your back. Excess weight will tire us out as well as strain our hearts, our lungs, our muscles and cause burning up of more energy than normally required to lead a good life and keep the body functioning at an optimum level. Fat and bulky people are conscious of their obese bodies and many of them have low self-esteem. On the other hand, proper body weight will increase your energy level almost immediately. Your self esteem will be heightened and you will feel healthier and happier. As you lose weight, you will feel a greater sense of personal power over your achievement and when you reach your ideal weight, you will be more effective in everything you do, apart from looking smart, slim and trim. Have a proper balanced diet as the food you eat has a tremendous effect on your vigour level throughout the day. Examine your diet and begin eating more foods that are better for you. Eat less of the foods that are not good for you. Changes in your diet, with emphasis on fruits and juices, can make you feel fresher, more alive, more alert, and filled with greater vitality. You should treat your body as a temple. The way to live to a happy, healthy age is to have proper intake of fruits, vegetables, nutritious foods, and whole-grain products. Once you form a habit of eating such food, you will be less willing to eat junk food. The *Bhagvad Gita* says that to have a good nature, you must eat juicy and fresh food. As far as possible, go in for fresh food and avoid tinned and greasy stuff. Determine your ideal weight and make a plan today not only to achieve it but to maintain it throughout your life. Along with good food, get into the habit of proper and regular exercise. Regular exercise will improve your digestion, and increase your vitality in physical, mental and emotional terms. The more energy you have, the better you will feel, and hence your output and efficiency will increase. Exercising will increase your flexibility, strength and endurance. The exercise can be yoga or running or walking or any game or sports you enjoy. Your aim should be gentle stretching of all your muscles and the exercise of your joints each day. The more you stretch your muscles on a regular basis, the more relaxed, coordinated, and in harmony you will feel. The day I do not exercise, I feel something missing from my life. This is apart from the stiffening of muscles. Exercises that build up your endurance level, including aerobic exercises, are the keys to a long and healthy life. Many people recommend that you should exercise at least three times a week for a minimum of 30 minutes. Others recommend five times per week. I would say that as you eat food every day and sleep every day, the same importance should be given to your physical fitness and exercises should be done every day for the rest of your life. I on my part, miss my exercise in the morning only when I have to catch a morning plane or train. Even then I try to make up in the evening. You can attain aerobic fitness by any method that suits you. It can be walking, running, swimming, cycling, rowing or cross-country skiing. The important thing is that this should improve your levels of health and energy. And it counts a lot. The results of such activities are cumulative. People who are healthy and energetic in their 50s and 60s had formed positive health habits in their 20s and 30s. People who live a long, healthy, happy life into their 80s are people who began planning for it long ago. They are the ones who maintained a reasonable discipline throughout their lives. Remember, every little effort counts in such achievements. Nobody lives forever. But why not live a quality life for the period God has given to us.

What Happens When You Think and Act Big?

Most people wish for big things to happen to them, which would bring them success and happiness and all the good things of life. They want a flourishing career, a fat income and the best of deals in life. For most people this will remain only wishful thinking. It is common to hear people say, "I wish that I had acted differently". It remains a wish, contrary to those who achieve big goals. Wishing has to be combined with acting big and taking big, bold actions. Only a combination of thinking big and acting big can make big things happen. When you think big, you can also conceive of bigger possibilities. It is the big picture which brings the big things to your life. A new world of possibilities opens up to you, leading to bigger achievements. Everything begins in the mind, it churns there, and produces a clear picture. New and better possibilities present themselves when you think big, as your mind would be looking for them. The small thinkers never see the big possibilities that come their way, even hit them on the head. A big thinker and doer is bound to go towards more possibilities. Noteworthy achievers do not waste their time with small time people, or on insignificant matters. They are always looking to work with people who want to play in bigger arenas. It is just like money attracting more money. People are attracted to you if you are willing to take a chance and act big. Be sure, big things will never happen to people with small dreams.

When we develop into big thinkers, and take big actions we can perceive big events taking place in our lives. The higher you think and the bigger bites you take, the add-ons will come along. Big things and big thinking are twin brothers and you cannot separate one from the other.

Big money comes to those who do big things and are big thinkers. Thinking small gets only small results. So think big, act big and the big money will start coming your way. Major contributions to life and society are made by dreamers who think big. No one ever becomes big accidentally. It comes from big thinking, and hard work. You cannot change the world without first changing yourself and without making a commitment to think bigger.

Starting right now, think bigger and act bigger to unlock the door to big things in your life.

To Feel Better, You Need to Think Better

This is a story about how one can work oneself into rage and failure. Once a salesman travelling in a car had a puncture on a dark, lonely road. He discovered that he had no jack to change the tyre. He saw a light in a farmhouse nearby and started walking towards it, so that he could borrow a jack. He started an imaginary discussion of a hypothetical situation.

He told himself that maybe no one will come to the door in response to his knocking and what if they do not have a jack. Suppose they do not lend him a jack, even if they have one. He starts thinking strenuously. The more his mind worked, the more agitated he became. By the time he reached the farm house, his thoughts had already turned him hostile and pictured for him a bleak and a negative scenario. When the farmer opened the door to inquire how he could help him, the salesman punched the farmer and shouted, "Keep your stupid jack." This story only brings home the point of what self-defeatist thinking can do to any individual.

People often say that nothing ever goes the way they plan and that they always mess up things. Such inner speech affects your life greatly. Our thoughts navigate our life, whether we like it or not. If your thoughts spell gloom and doom, that is exactly where you will end up. Negative words sabotage our confidence instead of offering support and encouragement. Simply put, to feel better, you have to think healthier. To do so, tune in to your thoughts and think optimistic, positive and constructive. If you keep a record, you will find that 30 to 50 negative thoughts cross your mind every hour or so, leading to your being tired and depressed. We need the tremendous energy we squander on being aware of imagined catastrophes. Feeling downcast could be due to your sending yourself negative messages. Listen to the words stirring up inside your head. Repeat them aloud or write them down, if that will help to imprint them on your mind. With practice, tuning in encouraging thoughts will become automatic. As you're walking or driving down the street, you can hear your own thoughts or you can put them on a tape recorder and play it in the car. Soon your thoughts will carry out your directive, instead of your being at their mercy. When this happens, you will see a change in your feelings and actions.

Leave behind destructive words and phrases. Think highly of yourself and ignore any suggestion of inferiority or low status. Never downgrade your job and, by its amplification, yourself. By using discouraging words and phrases, you can identify the harm you might possibly be doing to yourself. Most of the time, you will discover that the culprits are your own words. Once negative words are eliminated, you will notice a tremendous change for the better in your life and you will be on your way up the ladder. Block off all pernicious thoughts and short-circuit all negative communications as soon as they start entering your mind. However, this is easier said than done. You can use any technique, such as using the one-word command "stop"! You can raise your voice and give a command to your thinking process and mind to ban their entry. You have be forceful and tenacious. Do your best to accentuate the positive. Instead of thinking about possible failures, think of the wonderful time you had during the day. Recall how you laughed and your head will be filled with pleasant memories, and you will sleep peacefully. Prepare positive thoughts in advance. The Bible says : "Whatever is honourable ... whatever is lovely ... whatever is gracious ... think about these things."

Reorient yourself to newer thinking. Whenever you feel low, change the direction of your thinking, and your mood will brighten up. However tired a young man may be, a call for a late dinner from his fiancée will cheer him up and the fatigue is forgotten. A change in scene is both refreshing and cheering. Even aimless wandering makes you forget your problems. Once a week, I just go for window shopping to forget my preoccupations. I do not always buy something. It is just for a change of scene and routine. You can try it even now, just by going out and strolling. You will feel the difference. Practise the technique of going from distressing anxiety to an active, problem-solving framework. For instance, I hate to get caught in traffic jams. Even in the thick of a traffic jam, I keep on reading while my driver is busy negotiating through a maze of vehicles. This way, I ignore anxiety and spend the time usefully. By reorienting yourself, you can become skilled at seeing yourself and the world around you differently. If you think you can do something, you will increase your chances of doing it. Optimism will get you moving and depressing thoughts will bog you down. Never assume that there is no use in trying. Recall the achievements, for which you have been complemented. Convince yourself that it was and is the real you. Make this the configuration for your life. It should be an embodiment of you at your best. You will discover that a positive reorientation of your life, works like a magnet. Always believe that you will attain your goals. The poet John Milton wrote: "The mind ... can make a heaven of hell, a hell of heaven." If you think differently and positively you will get different and positive results.

Fast Forward

Says Norman Vincent Peale: "Believe in yourself! Have faith in your abilities! Without a humble but reasonable confidence in your own powers you cannot be successful or happy." We become what we think about most of the time. The most important part of every day is what you think about in the first few minutes of its commencement. So it is important to start your day right.

Start your day right

Take 20 minutes each morning to spend time with yourselves. Sit quietly and reflect on your goals and how you are going to plan the day for the achievement of the day's goals. Try to get up early. All successful men and women launched their upward journey to success by finding time for themselves and imbibing positive ideas. The first hour of the day sets the tone. The things that you do in the first hour, prepare your mind for the rest of the day. This establishes the course for the entire day. So try to get up early, plan for the day and review your achievements. Review your plans for accomplishing your goals. If necessarily, then do a mid-course correction and change your plans. The golden hour is the quiet time of your life. Using it effectively will produce the most productive results. During this time, think of better ways to accomplish your goals. Examine whether you are going about doing your work correctly or in a wrong way. Examine if you need to do it any differently from what you're doing right now. Contemplate the valuable lessons that you might have learned in the past, which might move you towards your goals.

Visualise your goals daily

Every day, calmly visualise your goal as a reality. Close your eyes, relax, smile, and see your goal as if it has already been achieved. Rewrite your major goals every day in the present tense, such as I am occupying X position or earning X amount of money or I am already worth X amount of money or my weight is X number of pounds. The exercise of writing and rewriting your goals daily is one of the most significant techniques for attaining success. Develop an attitude of unshakable confidence in yourself and in your competence to realise your goals. Everything ultimately boils down to building up and developing your belief system, so that you reach a point where you are absolutely convinced, that nothing can stop you from achieving what you aspire to achieve. We can develop such positive attitude by constantly accumulating success. On the road to success, every little bit, everything counts. No endeavours are ever in vain. Every extraordinary achievement is the result of thousands of ordinary triumphs that might not have won any recognition or appreciation. The biggest task for you is to concentrate your thinking single-mindedly on your goal. If you do so, then by the law of attraction, you will inevitably draw into your life the people, circumstances and opportunities you need to achieve your ambition.

Be clear in your thinking and mind. Aim at being financially independent. Financial success is the best form of success in life. Keep on trying to learn and keep on improving results in every area of your life. Your efforts should be to double your productivity. This is possible only if you learn how to simplify, streamline and decide exactly what you really want in every area of life. Once you achieve complete success over yourself and your thinking, you will become a centre for ideas and opportunities, which will enable you to become wealthy. It has worked for many people and it is bound to work for you if you begin today, right now, at this very minute. Think and talk about your dreams and goals as though they were already a reality. When you transform your thinking, you will revolutionise your life and put yourself effectively on the road to financial independence. Make it a habit every morning to plan your day. Take some time to think about and visualise your goals and how you can achieve them. This sets the theme for the whole day. At the same time, think of the valuable lessons you are learning each day as you move towards your goals. Be prepared to rectify your course and fine-tune your activities. Be absolutely positive and committed that you are moving rapidly towards your aim, no matter what happens temporarily to obstruct you. Just hang in there for some time more and you are bound to succeed.

Be Persistent

Often people feel frustrated or angry because they are not getting the things they want in their life, no matter what technique, strategy, or philosophy they use. The good news is that you can get out of such a situation by taking some very simple steps, and using some unusual techniques. You can follow these to make dramatic improvements in your life. Your life can become "Murphy's Law" in action, which says that what could go wrong will, in every part of your life, like your profession, your health and family front. But success has to come from within us. We have to conceive of and believe our 'Invisible Path' and then achieve with visible results, with our soaring attitude and self-confidence. If your self-esteem and self-confidence is low, and life has always been exhausting and difficult, it is time to create a breakthrough in your life. You need to discover why you have been so self-destructive in your relationships and why happiness and enjoyment of life have been eluding you. Being angry, frustrated, stressed out or being a workaholic is always exhausting. It results from the habit of pushing and pushing. Pushing, without rest or not pushing at the right time, does not generate a gentle and a peaceful life.

A feel good factor is morale boosting. Most of us realise it when our life swings in a particular direction. When we realise why it is so, then we also know exactly what to do, when we desire any change. All of us feel the same way. People wander from opportunity to opportunity looking for greener pastures. The following are different paths to a feel good factor.

Health and energy level

A friend told me that for about 20 years, no matter what he ate, how much he exercised, or how many doctors he consulted, or how many vitamins he took, he was always exhausted and tired. He would come from the office and the first thing he would do was lie down in bed. He always had constipation and had problems with his throat and digestive system. Now he has tonnes of energy to fuel him from 6 to midnight, or even longer, if he wants. His secret is as under. What matters most is what is happening in your body and what you think, what you feel, what you learn. What goes on inside of you is really much more important to you than what goes on outside of you. Ask yourself what you really want in your life. The answer can range from more money, a new job, a new house, a new car, to a new relationship. Further, you will get answers like peace of mind, more self-confidence, a sense of adventure, happiness, inner peace and love. It is important to seek changes in your life for getting a better job, more money, better relationships, and excellent health. It is equally important to focus on what is going on inside your thoughts, feelings, learning/growth and focus on the changes you want to make there too. It is our mind which is the captain of our life and the 'vision' that shapes our life. It manages all the details from behind the scenes to make sure that our life and work go on according to plan, on schedule, and towards the ultimate goal. The mind is an integral part of all of us. It works 24 hours a day, seven days a week, without taking a break, from behind the scenes to help us fulfil our life's objective.

Our mind is constantly sending signals to the world, asking for help on all kinds of projects on which we are working. It is also constantly monitoring the flow of other people's thoughts, like looking for opportunities to help you. It sends and responds to the messages of the unconscious part of our personality. It is the mind which can help you achieve goals and produce the results you want most. Your mind is one of the vital keys to creating a truly successful life in whatever way you may define it. A tea bag or tea leaves are just tea and hot water is just hot water. But you combine them to create a wonderful beverage. Similarly, if you combine your 'outer world' efforts with your mind and its directions in the 'inner world', you can create a similarly wonderful and refreshing result in your life. In our daily lives, we have telephones, cellular phones, fax machines, computers, the Internet, televisions, radios, and satellites. They link us all together and allow us to communicate our feelings and reactions with each other. In the absence of communication gadgets, our lives would be radically different, and it would need a different methodology to get anything done. So when this earth was formed originally, a very special invisible communications network was provided. This communications network connects all living beings together at the unconscious level. For instance, there is no rational explanation why a family members suddenly feels that something awful is going to happen before a tragedy befalls the family. Similar things have happened to many of us when we feel that something is going to happen before it has happened or when we guess, without even picking up the phone, who is calling us.

These experiences only show how we tap into this invisible network without consciously knowing about it. We are all 'connected' through this network, and through which we send messages to others unconsciously. Most of the time, we have no control over the process. All the time, messages flash back and forth at the unconscious level. People respond to our interaction and we respond to theirs. Just like in the 'real world', we discuss, negotiate and make agreements at the unconscious level. But it is also vital to realise that just about everything that happens in our life, is affected and shaped by the flow of messages in and out of the unconscious network that connects us. In order to optimise the results you produce in your life, you must learn how to work with your mind to consciously send and receive positively oriented messages through the unconscious network. No matter what results you want in your life, and no matter what you do at the 'conscious level', you must supplement your efforts by sending and receiving optimistic and encouraging vibrations through the unconscious network. An important thing to be remembered about the unconscious network is that unless your mind intervenes, all vibrations sent by the mind network will be taken literally by the people to whom they are directed or aimed. No one will question them, and may accept them literally. But it is for you to command yourself to be successful.

Aspire for Success

One of the reasons why so many people do not get what they ask for is, that they have doubts in their own minds. Quite often, we doubt whether we can achieve a particular objective. This conscious or unconscious objection is taken seriously by the mind. It interferes with our getting what we desire. Very often, we are not clear about what we want. The first thing is to be clear what you want from your life, in terms of your profession or job, family, friends and colleagues and what you think would make you happy, whether in terms of money or job satisfaction. In due course of time, you will notice that your life and the world take your desires literally to produce the results you want. There is an automatic, but imperceptible network that shapes what happens to us. The only condition is we have to be very clear about what we ask for, without a shred of doubt. Do not aspire for an ideal world and ideal conditions and then feel that you cannot achieve it as all such thoughts are taken literally and seriously at the unconscious level. If you do this, you will be ensuring that you do not get what you want. Have a dialogue with yourself to repel from your life all negative themes or the things you do not want. Never say negative things about yourself such as, I am a fool or an ass or I cannot get anything done right.

Such messages to yourself will have an impact on your life.

It is a mistake to keep repeating the same patterns over and over again, making the same mistakes repeatedly—like accepting the same kind of dead-end job, being mistreated or abused in personal or official relationships, making and losing money in similar circumstances. This happens because you have believed that anything better is not possible. So you go on accepting these unconscious negative messages and suggestions from your mind. The bottom line is that everything that happens in your life happens because of unconscious suggestions and beliefs fed into our unconscious network. You must constantly feed positive messages into your unconscious network and, 'filter' and respond to other people's unconscious messages so that they get translated into events and experiences, the way you want in your life.

Sending proper messages to your mind will eliminate feelings of frustration and confusion. It will give you a new strategy you can instantly activate instead of worrying about what to do next. This approach will help you understand and manage the unseen forces shaping your life, for getting what you want. There are no limitations to what you can achieve. This will dramatically increase the level of your happiness and personal satisfaction in your daily life. Consequently, it will also cause a dramatic decrease in the amount of fear or stress you feel. You will have more "ups" and less "downs" in your life. This way, you can advance your career quickly or create a new one that really meets your wants and needs, free yourself from guilt, anxiety, self-attack and worry, regardless of what your past was like. You will feel happier, more peaceful and confident, and be able to tell the difference between what you think you want and what you really want.

Organising Your Life and Home

Pick one room at a time for organising and cleaning it, till you are fully satisfied. An orderly working or living place not only has a fascination of its own, but is conducive to efficiency and promptness. As a matter of strategy, take the messiest place in your house or office, which even you avoid using. Mercilessly clear it of all clutter, and confusion. It is most important for your efficiency and existence. Organising should also include keeping your important papers like house, loans, taxes, job, and bank related information labelled, either in envelopes or transparent folders. I personally like to use transparent folders as it makes papers easy to spot and trace. The papers frequently used should be placed in an easily accessible place. Put everything, after you have used it in its fixed place or if necessary you can assign a new, more suitable place, to make your working smoother, and to have a feel good factor. This approach will ensure that you are not left fretting and searching desperately for information and records when you need them.

Remember family/friends/acquaintances

There are many festivals during which it is customary to give gifts, like Deepawali, New Year, Christmas or Raksha Bandhan. During the year, friends, associates, and family members help us in various jobs or on several occasions. It is a good idea to prepare a list of the special people in your life whom you might want to thank in the season of giving, for being useful and helpful to you. It can, and should include even the humble mailman or newspaper delivery boy, electrician and plumber.

Do something special for each of these people, whether it is giving a gift or sending a personalised note to each or a greeting card. This will win you their goodwill. The best way to keep a track of important events in your life such as birthdays, anniversaries and other recurring dates, plus any other known events already scheduled for the year is to highlight these special dates with a highlighter on a calender, so you can easily see what is coming up, and where your participation or presence is essential. Always keep appointments for activities which are essential for maintaining good health. These could be walking, bowling, skiing, ice skating, aerobics at the gym, basketball or swimming or anything which builds up endurance and enhances fitness. Form the habit of reading. This will take you on new journeys, into new worlds. Biographies or auto biographies of eminent people give you new insights. Update your contacts database from time to time. Contact your friends from time to time and confirm their mailing address, phone, fax, e-mail address and any other pertinent information. Make a list of people who have helped you in your profession, and periodically or at least once a year, send them a small gift or note of thanks for their help or invite them to a party. I personally host one party a year to say 'thank you' to all those who have helped me or have been otherwise useful to me. Keep a record of holiday tips, which might be useful for future reference. Giving helpful information is an excellent way to build trust and credibility.

Have Time for Your Life

Life is not as much about time management as it is about self-management. 'I have no time for my life' is the most common complaint. Although people say their family or their health is a top priority, their approach and time table does not reflect this. The 'inbox of their life' never empties and takes up all their time. Do not miss the good things of your life and keep on waiting endlessly for your to-do list to be completed. It is important to schedule time for your family and treat this time as sacred. When someone calls to make plans or asks you to do something during that time, simply smile and tell them you are busy, even though you may possibly feel some guilt doing so.

It is a fact that you cannot take out time for yourself and your family without cutting out a few things or denying others time. You are bound to disappoint others when you take time out for yourself or your personal commitments. Such people feel that they have the first right on your time. Do not feel guilty, as you are entitled to a life the way you want to live. You do not have to be apologetic for saying 'no' and living by your own new rules. You should not become slave to other people's agenda. It is more important to set limits to protect your peace of mind, your time and your commitments. You can turn the ringer off on the phone when you are doing vital work. Check your e-mail or voicemail only once or twice a day. You can tell people that you'll respond to calls and e-mails within four days to a week instead of the generally expected 24-hour period.

Stop juggling your time and start living, by dropping a few preconceived expectations from your existence. Do not try to please everyone. Do not try to do everything to absolute perfection. Do not sacrifice your life just to be known as a 'good girl' or a 'good boy'. Say goodbye to this role. It is bound to rob you of your life. A high-quality life involves what you remove from your life as much as what you add to it. So, instead of looking at what you'd like to add to your life in the New Year, equally focus on clearing out the old cobwebs. Clear out the clutter. Get rid of the obligations that make you feel aggrieved, indignant or bitter. Have the courage to defy the people who drain your energy, so that they do not come in your way. Dedicate yourself to self-care. Since most people usually know what they should be doing, it will be best to stop procrastinating and just do what is on the priority list.

Working smarter, and harder

The following tips will help in improving your effectiveness in the office.

1 Handle each piece of paper that comes to your table just once. Respond to it promptly, see whether it requires to be filed, or referred to others, or just consign to it to the dustbin. If you have to save it, then do so in the relevant file folder, so that you can trace it when you need it.
2 Throw out or sell to the *kabadiwala* papers and magazines that are more than three weeks old. You probably do not need the information on the Afghanistan war any more. [If you have put your phone on voice mail, after downloading, keep a written phone log of incoming calls with the person's name, number and message. To create space, you should clear the voice mail and delete the messages, after checking on your log when the call has been returned or handled. This way, you will avoid going through, and listening again, to several messages in order to trace the one which is most relevant to your work. If you handle e-mail, then read it once and promptly respond to it, or print it if you need to refer to it, and file it. Then delete the same from the inbox. Keep an 'emergency stash' in your desk (i.e. sewing kit, band aids, shoe polish, birthday cards or visiting cards). You will need them if there's a small crisis before a meeting or if you forget someone's birthday or anniversary.

What to do When Nothing Works

Every now and then, as we work to make our dreams come true, we will find ourselves tired, stuck and trapped. We may feel cornered and not know how to get on and move ahead. The following suggestions can help.

Believe and think positive

The road to success is RARELY always smooth. Any success has built-in challenges, and opponents. But with effort and dedication, you can surmount any difficulty. Another precondition is to stay positive and upbeat. Consistent positive thinking will help you achieve your goals.

Identify and change what does not work

We all know that if we knew what is not working, we would not be stuck with it. But the fact is that all too often we do not examine the situation as carefully and as extensively as necessary to locate the snags and hitches. When a bottleneck arises, check your road map, your goal, your priorities and the change in the scenario. Check whether you are you trying to do too many things at the same time and, thus, scattering your energy. Check whether you need any expert help or more information. The trouble is that pride or mere obstinacy prevents many of us, including myself, to ask for help when such help would solve all problems. We have to accept that there are people more brilliant and successful than us in the world. It is up to us to seek their assistance. Moreover, everybody is good at something. The trick lies in combining the available resources to achieve your goal. Take *some* action as any action is always better than no action. Even if it is at a time when you have absolutely no idea about what would be the best course. Sometimes guts and instincts guide rightly. Do not hesitate to change your plan, if any time you feel that you are on the wrong track. Take time to apprise yourself about what you are doing for moving towards your goal. Mid-term correction may somewhat change your schedule but it will ensure that you achieve your goals. When a difficult problem comes up, most people try to postpone it instead of meeting it head on. Such people succumb to inertia. Not facing or solving a problem or putting it under the carpet is no solution. It is fatal to success. It is the time to show your mettle by working harder from all angles.

Stretching to Your Outer Limit

Everybody in life wants to be happy and successful in doing whatever he or she wants to do or achieve. The word success emanates from a Latin word meaning "to follow". It is a future-oriented notion. If you do not decide where you want to go and what is your goal, you may not get there. It will be like a learner swimming at the same place in a swimming pool. Some kind of goal is essential, so that you can reach the place where you think you will find success. You cannot convince something to anybody who does not want to trust you or has no faith in you. You cannot even help somebody, who does not want to be helped. Vision is the catalyst that inspires us to move forward. It is not possible to have a one-size-fits-all formula for success. The following suggestions have been tried with success in the past by many. It is worth giving them a try. If you begin to apply them, chances are that you will be on the road to realising your goal.

Dare to dream, to believe that it is possible to achieve your ambition. Do not let unenthusiastic, unhelpful and pessimistic thinking discourage you. Be a dreamer, who will make the dream of his life a reality. Do not let your dream grow frosty and chilly. Stir it up and fan the flames of your expectation and ambition. Think big. Remember that everything begins in the heart and mind of a person. Every great achievement has its origin in the mind of one person. You should learn to believe in your dream. Think big and dream big. And work hard. The most successful people are usually those who work the hardest. While the rest of the world is watching television or eating in restaurants, the go-getter is busy working towards his goal. Every achievement, big or small contributes to your success. Each short-term task, multiplied by time, will equal your long-term accomplishments. If you work on your dream each day, eventually, you are bound to realise it. There is no substitute for hard work. Remember, the famous novel *War and Peace* by Leo Tolstoy was written in longhand, page by page. When you have achieved your goal and you are living your dream, be sure that you enjoy and relish it. To keep up your motivation, give yourself huge rewards when you realise your dream. After realising one dream, dream a little bigger one next time, but keep your dreams realistic. For example, if a person with heart disease believes that he can win an Olympics race, it can not come true. The same is the case of a person with arthritis believing that he or she will someday win a marathon race. However, if somebody with good education and a lot of grit believes that he can become a millionaire, it is not impossible. Every dream should be backed up by a plan; you get what you plan for. No dream just happens. You need to make it happen, by sitting down, on a regular basis, going through all of the details and planning a strategy for achieving it. Break your plan down into small, workable parts, with a time-frame for accomplishing each task. Help others along the way. There is a selfish reason in helping others, as in the process we improve ourselves and hone our skills. It is a kind of favourable self-perpetuation. A person talking to others on self-improvement or personality development is an equal beneficiary. While helping others, he realises sometimes that his own potential is unbeatable. Everybody has a tremendous potential for success, but unfortunately, quite often we run into self-centred, self-delusional, pessimistic and basically lazy people with a total lack of ambition. This inhibits us from expanding our potential for achievement. However, *it is possible* to achieve whatever you want, and

have a success-type personality—one that will empower you to set and achieve goals throughout your life. The only condition is that you have to free your creative potential and be able to express your real self, so that you can deal effectively and appropriately with the environment and reality, and get satisfaction from realising your goals. For this you have the self-image of a go- getter, who can anticipate what skills and qualities will be indispensable for success in the years to come ahead. Matiz has described Success as under.
- Sense of direction,
- Understanding,
- Courage,
- Charity,
- Esteem,
- Self-confidence and
- Self-acceptance.

Always keep your mind filled with self-confident and bold thoughts. Never allow any negative thoughts to creep in, as they will destroy all your yearning for success. One important input for this is to carefully select your reading material, and put only positive thoughts in your mind. It is one way to interact with great minds and intellectual giants. Find out how others achieved what you want to achieve and follow in their footsteps.

If we continually say something to ourselves we tend to believe it. The more you tell yourself, the more you will believe. If you share your dreams with others, you are obliged to exert hard to achieve them. Share your dreams and aspirations for success with your friends and loved ones who will not make fun of you.

Develop Success Habits

The following are the success habits which should be cultivated by all of us. If you want to be successful, you should not put off things. Get into the habit of prioritising your daily tasks. You should differentiate between what you must get done, as distinct from what you think you should get done. Have some sort of task logic system. The system or method should keep you focussed and on target with your goals. Keep an idea book or some other notebook. Set a realistic date for acting on each so that you are not overwhelmed by numerous ideas.

Keep your promises

If you make a promise to yourself and to others, keep it at all cost. Accomplish what you say you are going to do, and when you say you are going to complete it. Back up your expression with your deeds and create confidence by being dependable.

Brainstorm regularly

For every problem there is a solution. Acquire the habit of thinking for better performance. Obstacles and problems should not deter you from achieving your goal. If one approach does not work, another will. Be persistent as well as creative. Do not admit defeat over the first debacle.

Challenge yourself to excel

We are all tempted to take the easy way out, but don't do it. Do not be afraid to implement what your spirit, mind and heart counsel you to do. For example, if your heart and mind are not happy doing something, you should consider not doing it. If you insist, then one course is to be adapted to the situation and be happy, otherwise, sooner or later, you will be unhappy with your choice and no closer to realising your real goal. Challenge yourself and discover new strengths and expand your comfort zone. Suddenly, your goal will not seem that far off after all.

Stay focussed

Keep reminding yourself of your aspirations and your main concerns. Respect your deadlines. Keep goal reminders on written cards, on your table, in your wallet, in your office computer, on the kitchen bulletin board, and other places where you will see them regularly. Whenever you are faced with the question of what is the most important thing you should be doing right now, see your goal reminder cards.

Always be realistic

Have a firm grip on truth. Your success is up to you and it is in your hands. Do not wait for success to happen. Assume complete responsibility for your success from beginning to end. Do not blame others when things go wrong. Acknowledge that your success is in your own hands, of your choosing, at all times.

Try your best

Never be afraid of hard struggle and sweat. Sacrifice is necessary to reach your goals. But do not work yourself to complete exhaustion. It does neither you nor your objective any good. So you should also know your limits. Else, you are likely to make mistakes and errors of judgment. Common sense should be balanced with steady efforts.

Make it fun

Show enthusiasm at every step of the journey of your life and love what you are doing. You have to take many tedious little steps to reach your goal. Why not make it fun, by converting the entire exercise into an interesting game. Try to surpass your goals by staying motivated and by keeping your eye on the accolade and honour. Reward yourself for completing the tricky things in time.

Always keep learning

We must acknowledge that our success is a learning and happening event. Our mission should be to discover what works, what does not, and why. This will not only lead to achievement of the goal, but also enable us to learn. We should all the time be building up our success muscles. Most importantly, never be afraid to learn from your mistakes. There is no harm in admitting that you have made one. At the same time, do not be afraid to learn from your success process.

Do not hesitate to ask for help

Be graceful enough to realise that you cannot do all things by yourself. Ask, delegate, or hire others wherever you need help, to realise your dreams. Be smart enough to realise that you do not always have to start from the beginning. Focus on making your unique contribution to whatever you are doing. For this, work intelligently and be on the lookout to automate, streamline, and generate new ideas.

Cut your losses

Don't be afraid to start from the beginning when something does not work out the way you want. At some intervals, say once in a month or periodically conduct a simple cost-benefit analysis of whether you are near achieving your goal, and the cost of the time, effort, and/or money. If you are not succeeding, think of what to do next. Salvage any lessons from the experience for use next time.

Always believe in yourself

Your success must ensue from within. You must first have faith that you can achieve your goals, even before you attempt them. Dynamically picture yourself as accomplishing your goal. Have this yearning on an unrelenting basis. Have a big vision and keep it crystal clear by first having confidence in yourself and in your ideals.

6
The Requirements for Creativity

Develop Health Goals

If we do not take time for maintaining our health and fitness, we will have to give time later for treating illness and regain health. Health is the area which most people tend to value the least, until they do not have it anymore. When health is gone, most would be willing to pay any amount to purchase a few more years of quality living. The problem is, you cannot buy good health. It is not available at any price. We have to learn to set our own health goals for our life, and for the current year. A health plan has to be worked out in advance – what has to be done each month, each week, and each day – to reach the goal. Health goals need to fit in with one's daily schedule and be a continuous exercise.

Energy is Basic to Any Achievements

Most successful people have very high levels of energy. Energy is the fuel without which no achievement is possible. There is a direct relationship between energy levels and levels of achievements. No perpetually tired or burnt-out person can achieve anything worthwhile in life, as without basic energy, no enthusiasm or drive is possible. On the other hand, energetic, positive, forward-moving individuals get joy and fun in their lives and are generally ahead in the race. The human body is like any other machine. The only difference is in its method of charging and working. It is recharged by different types of batteries. Each night we recharge our body batteries by sleep or rest of six to eight hours. We have been steered to believe that there is only one kind of energy, which is replenished by rest or sleep at night, as well as by rest during the day. Truly speaking, apart from physical energy, we also require emotional and mental energy. These are different types of energy, but at the same time, they are meticulously and systematically in harmony with and dependent on, each other. All three types of energy, are necessary for peak performance. Physical energy is natural vitality, basic to everything in life, including emotional and mental energy. Physical energy, used for physical exertion, is necessary for earning our livelihood. To that extent mental and emotional energy are different from the primary energy applied by men and women to earn their living by the sweat of their brow.

Though mental and emotional energy do not deal with THE SWEAT OF YOUR BROW, neither is possible without physical energy, hence there are no contradictions between the three types of energy.

The source of enthusiasm

Emotional energy generates enthusiasm and excitement and lends sparkle to the life of an individual. Without this energy, you cannot experience feelings of love, happiness, and joy. It is essentially emotional energy that makes life enjoyable for all of us. In fact, anything you say or do is determined, to a great extent, by an emotion, either positive or negative.

Intellectual or mental energy is the energy of ingenuity, inventiveness, originality and resourcefulness. It is required for problem-solving and decision-making. Mental energy is required for writing reports, floating ideas and discussing and presenting proposals, planning your time during the day and week, and learning new things. Mental energy is a major determinant of the quality of life. This is what enables us to learn building self-esteem, setting goals in every aspect of life, re-programme our mind for success and unlocking our mental powers. Learn to conserve your energy. Many people fail to attain their potential in life and work, because they drain their emotional or physical energy over the wrong priorities. Thus, they have very little energy left over for intellectual activities. Usually, such people burn up their emotional energy on negative emotions. Negative emotions are like fire. They burn up the energy so quickly that very little is left at the end of the day for thinking positively and constructively.

One five-minute, uncontrolled outburst of anger not only burns up plenty of emotional and mental energy, but also upsets our routine for the next one to two hours. Anger also puts you out of the mood to work and achieve your aim. We should strive to continually stay calm and positive, and work smoothly and efficiently, with the sole objective of having more mental and emotional energy to do the things that are most important in our life. To tackle such situations, we should take time to identify the different ways that exhaust our levels of physical, emotional and mental strength and how can we improve in each sphere. All energy is generated by fuel and the fuel comes from nutritious food which keep physical energy at peak levels. Physical energy is the key to all vigour and strengths. Emotional energy should be conserved by being more relaxed and optimistic even in the face of problems and disappointments.

The more energy you have, the happier and more productive you will be. This will enable you to set suitable goals in every area of life and help you in discovering your personal area of excellence. You will be able to release your inborn originality and take charge of your thinking. You will be able to overcome obstacles or difficulties and nothing will stop your from achieving your goals. This will automatically mean more promotions and more income.

Overplan your day

Overplan your day by 45 per cent more than you think you can complete. You will take advantage of Parkinson's Law, which states that "a project will tend to expand with the time allocated for it". If you have one thing to do today, it will take you all day. If you have only two things to do, you will get both done. If you have twelve things to do, you may not get twelve done but you may get nine done. Having a lot to do compels us to get focussed. In fact, having a lot to do automatically makes us better time manager. We are more focussed, we suffer interruptions less, we naturally delegate more, etc. "If you want something done, give it to a busy person" so goes a saying.

Work Culture and Performance Improvement

There is a saying that "one cannot run faster than the train on which one is travelling". This needs to be perennially kept in mind while discussing work culture and performance improvement. No matter how one plans performance enhancement and participation in a job, it is ultimately the team work and the work culture prevailing in an organisation that determines final achievement. Performance models, designs, structures and processes provide the framework. The culture of an organisation determines the actual proficiency in the implementation of any plan or task. Any worthwhile performance improvement measure should be put in place, or at least there should be some operational parameters, who is to supervise the same, and at what level they would be located. The purpose of the exercise should be to achieve the organisational goals, missions and values. The issues of vision, missions and goals need to be given paramount attention and should not be left ambiguous. Vague goals lead to vague results. Nothing in life is immutable. Theories and methods of working can be refined and improved. But environmental considerations play a great role in determining the shades, the colour and the thrust of the achievements.

At one time in our country, socialist theories and nationalisation were the buzzwords. Now there is an obsession with privatisation, liberalisation and free enterprise. Going headlong in one direction can do little to exclude the reality that competition can be both fair and unfair. The sooner it is realised that the markets cannot be perfect and static, the better it would be for the country. In due course of time, competition can overtake the enthusiasm of the proponents of the market economy. Under these circumstances, it is important to keep under strict control the tendencies of unresponsiveness and irresponsible and unfettered use of powers in any organisational scheme of things, whether in the private or public sector. The question arises: where does all this leave us as far as the system improvement module is concerned?

Here are some suggestions for putting things in the right perspective and focus. The performance improvement measures in both government and private sector are very often undertaken as if governance is a somewhat undisputed enterprise. This is conceptually unsustainable, as governance, as a process, is as vibrant as life. There is a clear need to divide one's career into viable segments. For each segment, we should outline a desirable profile. It is a difficult and tall order, because at each age and every position we hold in life, we need to outline for ourselves the kind of person we want to be. Then we need to work backwards to decide as to what kind of calibre and competence is required to reach that level. To be conscious of what we want to be is the first step towards reaching our goals. The same principles are required for developing the careers of others in any organisations. Of course, running a huge organisation or for that matter, even a small one, would further require identifying its purpose and the resources it can command.

Continuity, connectivity of competency and personality profile, while moving from one stage to another, and indeed throughout one's entire career, as well as the career of others working under or with us, are absolutely crucial. Organisations divide the careers of their employees into different segments, depending upon the competence, profile and qualifications of the individuals, so that round pegs are not fitted in square holes. However, the basic professional characteristics and traits remain the same in all individuals, though some variations of range and depth can be caused by training and exposure to new ideas and environments. Performance measurement and improvement can be effected in professional setting. Improvement in personal characteristics needs consistent and continuous efforts. Nevertheless, coordination between and among the stages of one's career should always be kept in view, both by the individual concerned, as well as his organisation, so that the skills gained in one area are not lost or unutilised or underutilised. This would have to be fitted in the organisational goals, missions and values. It would require articulation in clear terms, so that each individual is clear about his role and the inputs that are expected from him in terms of performance and development measures.

Lack of the above factors is the chief reason for the failures of the "Government", which itself is a kind of an umbrella term, under which many macro and micro organisations, often pulling in different directions, exist. This is the reason why people jocularly say that government work is nobody's work. There is no urgency to set or achieve any goal because in the Government, the letter of the rules is more important than achievement of any objective or the spirit of the rules. There is hardly any accounting for performance, or for improving one's competence. In fact, my experience shows that people who have trod on somebody's toes, or are not wanted elsewhere, are sent for training. Some people get overtrained and under utilised in the bargain and the result is that organisations suffer.

Performance improvement is possible only through performance planning, performance feedback, coaching, counselling and, finally, performance appraisal. Performance improvement systems vary from place to place and from organisation to organisation. But in the Government, it consists of Annual Confidential Reports, Performance Appraisals, Performance Management, and Integrated Performance Management. Each has its own *raison d'être* and serves a useful purpose. It is open to each organisation, to make a conscious choice or choices. But conceptual clarity is a must. No performance improvement system is either possible or workable unless one is clear about the job substance and configuration. This corresponds to management of an expert system. Nevertheless, for effective functioning, standards need to be evolved and monitoring systems put in place. For each job, it is important to list the inputs so that the required output may be anticipated.

All performance, including individual performance, is bound to be affected by the approach of the team of which one is a member. Wherever any work requires team work and not individual performance, an integration of collective performance and individual performance capabilities would need to be established. The concepts and techniques of performance or accomplishment improvement get amplified in every age. The performance improvement systems require a second look and restructuring, depending on the parameters of design, process, structure, interpretation and implementation with the constant objective of introducing new improvement features from time to time, appropriate to the aims and goals. This may appear difficult but is an achievable target. Any performance evaluation is as significant as the people managing it want to be.

For succeeding in life, we must learn to adjust to changing times and still hold unchanging principles. Every week, for five or six days a week, most people go to work either in their own business or for someone else. Either way, each person is investing a lot of TIME and ENERGY, helping to make a business or a profession or a job succeed. It is important then to ask a question as why should it be so. You must have a reason for doing what you want to do. The PURPOSE of any business is the reason for its being. The purpose should not be confused with the goals and business strategy. A purpose is long-lasting. A purpose is never fully attainable. It is something you always work towards. Knowing your purpose is not a small issue. Research has shown that lasting businesses or enterprises have a clearly defined purpose. The purpose of all giant organisations has not changed since their inception.

Their purpose has always included some contribution or value the business will make to the people living in the country or the community. The purpose can include the advancing and applying of technology for the benefit of the public or making some technical contributions for the advancement and welfare of the community or for solving problems or doing something innovative.

There has to be some driving force behind any worthwhile enterprise. The way to understand an organisation is to know its purpose and yours too, in it. It is important to remember that you are not going to create the purpose. It already EXISTS within every organisation One way of finding out your organisation's purpose is to ask the following questions:

1. Why is the organisation existing?
2. How can people be made interested in its product or services? Does it help people in leading a fuller life? Do they want to remember important times in their lives, because of what your organisation is doing for them?

The advantage of knowing the purpose of your organisation is the contribution you can make in the lives of the people who use its services. This will enable you to evaluate your services or your business or profession from your customer's or client's point of view. It will also open for you new OPPORTUNITIES you may not have envisaged. Knowing the reason for the existence of a business or a job gives us a goal to work towards. So it is important to discover the purpose of your business. If everyone in your organisation knows the purpose, they will be more focussed, more motivated and more successful. And if your organisation thrives, you also automatically thrive.

It is considered wrong and discourteous to ask for or decline gifts. We accept whatever gifts are given to us with thanks, though later we may feel that the gift is of no use. There is no harm in requesting that either no gifts be given on an occasion, or if at all anything is to be given, it should not take up space because of space constraint. Many of us have more 'stuff' than we really need now or will ever need. Yet some people feel compelled to give us even more stuff on any conceivable excuse, including when they return from a holiday. It is one way of increasing social interaction.

You can let people know casually or even formally as to what kinds of gifts you would prefer. Gifts like tickets to a movie or a play, the zoo, or a musical are "experience" gifts. Gifts like bank gift certificates or gift vouchers to a restaurant, a spa, or for other services, are another option. Consumable gifts such as a fruit basket, a bottle of wine, or cakes, pastries and biscuits are other useful gifts that do not add to clutter.

You too could start giving similar "non-cluttering" gifts to friends and family members. The better course would be to ascertain their wishes. On the birthdays of children, I invariably ask them what kind of gift they would like. Mostly, I give them money and let them purchase what they want.

This way you can minimise the clutter in your home. As artist William Morris said: "Have nothing in your houses that you do not know to be useful or believe to be beautiful." By following good habits throughout the year, you can lead a clutter-free life. It is better to involve your kids to make room for gifts. This is also a way to teach them that they will soon be surrounded by clutter if they keep accumulating and do not clear things out.

Maintenance and Upkeep

Organisation is basic to success, whether it is running your home or office. It is something that requires a constant effort. Reorganisation is like renewing oneself and bringing forth new zeal and enthusiasm. There is a great pleasure in leading a well organised life. It boosts one's morale and energy. It is up to each one of us to make a fresh start by thoroughly cleaning and organising our home and work place. If you do not do it regularly, the disorganisation will overtake you. The trick is to make the process both manageable and enjoyable. For this take steps for planning in advance. List the areas you want to clean. When deciding what needs to be done, imagine that you are putting your home up for sale, and you want it looking unsurpassed for potential buyers. Make it a point to give it a good whitewash, and arrange to have places like closets and kitchen cabinets cleaned. Prioritise your list. It will be realistic not to aim to get everything done at once, and on the same day. So determine in advance which areas you want to deal with first. Think about which section of your working place or home frustrates you the most. Decide what you want to do first.

Set a deadline for cleaning each area. Making a priority list and starting acting upon it is a great starting point towards cleaning and organising. This list is simply a reminder of what you intend to do and is not a substitute for action. Assign a deadline for each area and each item. This is one way, to translate your intentions into practical work. Plan appropriately for the areas, depending upon the season and timing. You may wish to store the winter clothes at the onset of summer and vice versa for the summer clothes.

Break down each area into less significant areas or projects. This will enable you to map out the specific things you are going to work on in each area. It will also help you to identify tasks that can be accomplished in a short span of time. For example, you can take up cleaning and organising the bedroom area into the dressing room part, bookshelves, closet, etc. This way, you can focus on specific items during each organising session, and make the assignments seem less daunting.

Get your family to help you in cleaning the clutter. They will also keep things clean and organised. To keep them enthused, you can allocate to each family member one of the smaller projects within each room (e.g., one person can clean the music system or TV, another the bookshelves, another the closet, etc). Have everyone sort out his or her clothing and put the same in order. Get rid of items that are worn out, those which no longer fit and those you do not want to use. You can even donate, or sell the items that don't fit, but are otherwise in excellent condition. This will generate and often open up a lot of storage space. While working, you can make it fun with music on, to keep everyone's drive and vitality sparkling. You can have contests, like who can fill up the most garbage bags and have suitable rewards for the winners. Once the house is clean and organised, treat yourself and your family to something you or they like to do. For heavy items like carpets or rug washers, make appointments with professionals, preferably before you start your clean up campaign. Making these appointments will help you commit to getting started, and keep to your part in the cleaning of the house or your workplace.

Schedule time on your calendar to work on decluttering periodically, say once a week for smaller projects, and once a month for bigger projects. Do it regularly, and then assess the results. However, do not try to get everything done at one go. You will feel exhausted and burnt out. Be sure to have on hand all the supplies you will need for cleaning up, like a ladder or boxes for sorting things so you can continue working uninterrupted once you get started. Work progressively towards your goal of decluttering. Make sure that you meet the earlier established deadlines. If you find yourself losing resolve, then take a break to take stock of the work you have done and schedule your next cleaning session with easier tasks, or even think of hiring help.

Don't just clean the stuff which is causing clutter. Consider also whether you really need some items. Use the cleaning time to determine whether you really need to hang on to the belongings that are cluttering your life. If you are not using them, put them in one of your sorting boxes, marked "Donate" or "Sale", or just give away or throw them out. Be sure that whatever items are put in the "Donate" or "Sale" category boxes are actually removed within a week. If you want to sell, then think of planning a garage sale.

Once you've taken the measures to clean and organise an area, make it a point to maintain it that way. Put away things when you have finished using them. Clean up a mess as soon as it occurs. Develop a regular cleaning schedule, so that you can finish everything, bit by a bit, over a period of time. Do not aim to clean the entire house at once, do it in stages. After you have done it, take time to enjoy the energised look of your clean and organised home or workplace.

Simplify and Streamline Your Life

Take fifteen minutes a day for reflection. It is best to do this first thing in the morning, when the house is quiet and there is no disturbance. Think about the big picture of your life, what you want to achieve. After your reflection, make a list of five things you really enjoy doing, and five things that deplete your dynamism and enthusiasm. Make an effort to be really innovative and ingenious. Farm out or get out of your system all the activities which enfeeble you. Try to stop them and if you cannot do it now, plan to do the same gradually. Your goal should be to do in your life what you like doing. Do not waste time on activities that sap your energy.

If you really want a rationalised and reorganised life, the first thing to do is to get out of any debt, including the debt on consumer items. Having a life full of debt and no savings or investment is a life of insecurity and uncertainty, with no choice, except to keep on working whether you like your job or not. It is better not to have credit cards and spend only when you can afford to or, keep only one credit card and make sure that you pay all your bills every month. Absolute discipline is a must for an independent and trouble-free life. Try not to be in debt to other people, though all of us are indebted to God for all his blessings.

Streamlining your living place means having an efficient, attractive, welcoming, and clutter-free house. You can start with one room, or one drawer at a time and get rid of everything you do not need or use really and truly regularly. Clutter is a huge energy drainer. When you go for buying something ask yourself whether you really need it, will it be of any use to your life, and worth the extra hours you will need to clean it or even pay for it. Everything you bring into your house means more clutter unless you need it immediately or will use in the near future.

Business Week magazine once said: "We're the quirky civilisation that rides elevators to the second floor and buys electronic stair steppers to condition our thighs. We drive to convenience stores and hurry back to our treadmills. Yes, we rely on machines to save us from working, then buy other machines to save our bodies from the terminal flab." Park your vehicle a block away and walk to make your purchases or do your errands. You can join a physical fitness class, but it should be in addition to your exercises in the normal course of your day. Buy fresh food, rather than precooked food. It is less expensive and better for your health. Eat your food the way nature intended you to, that is fresh from the fields, and you will be rewarded with health and vitality.

You must learn to start saving and investing. Money may not bring you happiness, but you can never be comfortable without it. If you do not know much about investing, you can take advice from a financial consultant so that you can get your money working for you, not against you. Saving will enable you to be independent, at present as well as in retirement. Enjoy the simple pleasures of life. Read, play a board game, watch sunset, take a luxurious hot water bath. Even a 15-minute hot bath provides wonderful relaxation after a hectic day. Eat at least one meal with your family. Invite a friend over once in a fortnight. Give a touch of class by having a candle light dinner on your own dining table. Always protect your time, for its better utilisation. Don't say yes when you really want to say no to invitations. Try to respond to every invitation by saying, "Let me check my diary or calendar and I'll let you know tomorrow." That will give you time to think carefully, about whether you should accept the invitation or not.

Why are People So Mean?

It is one thing to show your disapproval to someone at his face and another to smile at them and later tear them apart behind their backs. If you must fault someone, have the graciousness and thoughtfulness to do so face to face. Do not stoop to gossiping. Be mature and practise honesty in your relationships. For example, if one of your friends has a bad habit of denigrating everyone, why not be assertive and calmly point this out to him instead of competing with him in conduct or feeling resentful about it. And if you are a real friend, why not take this person aside and talk to them about how his behaviour is affecting your friendship. If you are honest with yourself, you will realise that your negative feelings about other people often reflect your own insecurities and fears. More often than not, the quality of our relationship with others replicates how we feel about ourselves. There is an emotional poison generated by negative behaviour or holding on to your anger. It does not do you any good to sulk or brood over someone's behaviour. Without letting the concerned person know that you are upset you are not going to change anything. You have to be brave and tackle how you are feeling so that you can stop negativity affecting your life. When dealing with difficult people, you have the choice of avoiding and ignoring them, or letting them know how you feel so that you can come to some sort of understanding or solution. It all depends on what influence such a person has on your life, your relationship with that person, and the importance you want that person to have in your life. In other words, when dealing with a difficult person your aim should be to understand, forgive, and move towards your own goals without any waste of time. You should rise above hurtful behaviour and get on with living your life to the fullest.

If you have nothing nice to say to someone or about someone, then it is better to keep your mouth shut. When we want to hurt someone, we just attack their weak points. If at any time you are tempted to stoop to hurt someone, think again, and again. Hurting someone, just because you can, will not make you a better person. If anything, it will show you as a small, mean, and petty person. No matter how much you dislike anybody, never sink so low that you behave without honour or scruples. When we deliberately set out to hurt others, we hurt ourselves most of all. To harm others, even one's enemies, harms you, it takes away some essential element from your self-respect and self-image.

Do You Hope Bad Things Will Happen Only To Others

It is one thing not to like someone, but quite another to talk other people into disliking them as well. What can you do in a situation like this? Stand up for the victim, if he is your friend and is not there to defend. Let the critic himself know that you are averse to his talking about your friend this way. Do not spend hours being angry about anybody's behaviour. You will end up wasting just a lot of time on negativity. This takes away joy from your life. Do not give any difficult relationship that much power over your life and your happiness. There are a number of lessons to be learned from those around us. If you find yourself repeating unsatisfactory relationship patterns, perhaps it is time for personal change. You must ask yourself how you are contributing to the unfulfilling relationships. Because ultimately, it is for you to lead your life. Change has to begin with you.

It is generally easy to slip into negativity, your own or someone else's. You need not remain this way. It is up to us to rise above our most unpleasant weakness and become better people.

Every Problem Has a Built-in Solution

The first step in getting anywhere is to decide what you want to achieve, or where you want to go. Set targets as your destination. Make your aim something that will call for the fullest use of all your abilities, for hard work, courage and perseverance. You will need all these qualities if you want to achieve your goals. Try to picture yourself as you intend to be in ten years time.

You must not set your sights low. Aim high. Have an ambition which will tax your abilities to the full. Begin with a list of your assets and make a proper assessment of yourself. Examine the qualities you have acquired from your family and background. However humble your origin may be, it has contributed something to your character and experience. Try to identify that something unique and make the best use of it. Similarly, examine in detail your education, experience, skills, health or age or maturity, money, and friends, who may help you in achieving your goals. Everybody has some unique quality which can contribute to whatever he wants to achieve. No characteristic in any human being is too small. It is only your personal assets which can fulfil your ambition. Be bold in deciding your goals, aims and ambition. Your inner strength will come to your help. Be helpful to others and do things for the general benefit of the mankind.

Talk in a way that shows confidence and a winning attitude. Our attitudes are revealed in our speech. By controlling our conversation, we can influence our attitudes. Your conversation reflects your state of mind. By the physical action of talking, you can determine what your mind shall convey now and in the future. It is the actions which create the thoughts. Whatever you say today will create in you the person you will be in the days to come. If you want to be self-confident, talk in a self-confident manners. To like someone, talk as though you already like him. To develop a winning attitude, talk in a victorious and successful manner. Consciously decide what is most important for achieving your goals. This should be done every day. Concentrate on where you want to arrive. Each human being whether poor or rich is given the same number of hours every day. The only way to make the optimum use of time is to use it wisely. For being successful, you must learn, to use every spare moment, including the time spent on a journey and the time between the meetings, purposefully.

Nothing will help more in strengthening your self-confidence than a clear-cut goal and destination. Your journey to your specific destination may take days, months and years. It is patience which will stand you in good stead. Often, you will have to be content with the small gains which will lead you to final achievement. Your aim should be to develop self-confidence. It will enable you to act as if you are afraid of nothing. There is great power in setting up and moving towards a definite goal within realistic time limits. It is far greater than muscle power. You should not allow anyone's opinion to affect you, if it does not harmonise with your definite aim in life. Success consciousness can be instilled into any mind. Your mind should picture a desired goal. Your success consciousness and positive thinking will lead you towards it.

For making self-suggestion or auto suggestions effective, you must not think of the unwanted things. Concentrate only on the things you want. *"Keep your mind on the things you want and off the things you don't want."*

7
Organise Your Work and Home Life

Ways to Score Points with Your Wife

Everybody wants a happy a life. The way to have a happy life is to make your spouse happy. The following are a few simple ways which can help:

1. On returning home after work, find her and before doing anything else, give her a hug.
2. Ask her about her day.
3. Bring her flowers or other gift items as a surprise.
4. If she generally makes dinner, but is not inclined to do so, or has been busy otherwise, offer to cook, if you know cooking or take her out, or get food from a restaurant of her choice. Treat her as a girl friend, exactly in the way, you did at the beginning of your relationship.
5. When you are going to be late, call and let her know that you will be late and tell her why.
6. When you are going to be out of town, leave a phone number where you can be reached and then call to tell her that you have arrived safely. If you can afford it, carry a mobile phone so that she can always be in touch with you, and contact you in case of an emergency.

7 When she wants to talk to you at home, put down the magazine or newspaper you are reading or turn off the television if you are watching it and give her your full attention.
8 Keep the bathroom floor clean and dry after taking a bath or shower. Give her a minimum of four hugs a day. Psychologist call this reassurance support.
9 Make it a point to cuddle or be affectionate frequently without being sexual. Don't answer the phone at intimate moments or if she is sharing some vulnerable or hurt feelings.
10 Support her when she's upset with someone. Bring home her favourite food or dessert.
11 Generally go to sleep together and get into bed at the same time.
12 Get tickets for a movie or the theatre, ballet, symphony, opera, or some other performance she likes and go out at least once in a fortnight, if not more often.
13 Carry a picture of her in your wallet and update it from time to time. It will make her feel good.
14 Call from work to ask how she is or to share something exciting or to just say "I love you" from your private cabin, if you have one, not from a public phone.

Making a Lasting Impression

If you think you are "open-minded", then try to catch yourself if you are being intolerant of someone with a different viewpoint. Says Aristotle, "I count him braver who overcomes his desires than he who conquers his enemies; for the hardest victory is the victory over self. The only way to get the better of an argument is to avoid it. Generally, nobody can plan encounters or situations that will create lasting impressions. However, we can try to be more aware of our behaviour and the influence it may have. Starting today, right now, we should realise that every interaction we have with others is precious. There are no ordinary moments in our lives. Each moment is extraordinary. Keep this in mind, and consciously choose to be honest and kind. Put in your best efforts at all you do, at all times. Cherish your visions, your dreams and your ambitions. They are the blueprints of your ultimate achievements. Nobody ever finds himself magically in the right place at the right time, where everything just falls into place. It's not just luck. It is not something that just happens by accident or luck. It is up to you to make it happen, by your conscious efforts. You have to learn to tap your natural ability to abort the things that make you uncomfortable and drag you down, leading to regret and remorse.

So, the next time you are going to do something, either for yourself or for others, ask yourself: What action should I take right now to make sure that my behaviour and conduct will have a lasting effect on others? This is not to say that we can be perfect all the time. There are, and will always be, times when all of us behave in ways that are less than perfect, not something to be proud of. However, if you realise the impact of your day-to-day conduct, you will find yourself making different and better choices. I would like to share here something interesting which I learnt from a taxi driver.

One morning in Delhi, I caught a taxi to go to the airport and during the ride, the driver suggested some RULES for SUCCESS, which are as under.
1. Pay your bills and keep your credit. Never delay paying your bills.
2. Obey the laws even if nobody is watching.
3. Remember God is watching over, and caring for you. Trust that everything happens for the best. God is in charge and He looks after everybody in His creation.
4. Avoid lazy, crooked people and criminals.

Organise Your Work and Home Life 139

5. Make your workplace as comfortable as you can, just like your home.
6. Love and honour your boss and the people you come in contact with.
7. Keep your promises at all costs.
8. Mind your own business and do not dabble in the affairs of others.

You should set your goals and live your dreams. Do not wait until you could get something better. Seize every opportunity you get and be happy with what you have. Live enthusiastically and give life your best shot. This is the only marvellous preparation for a better tomorrow! Wealth demands sacrifice, discipline, and hard work. For happiness, you have to follow simple rules. The first one is always live well below your means. The last one is, choose your profession wisely. Appreciate the ripple effect. It is just not possible to fathom the consequences of the lasting impressions we make on others or other events. We affect all with whom we eventually come in contact. This may sound incredible, but it is not an exaggeration. Our parents, teachers and colleagues help to shape our character, which in turn affects the way we deal with people. Similarly, other people, whom I have met, may have been affected. They may have passed along those values to others they had met, making it an endless cycle. Thus, there is no small action in this world. Any simple act can truly change the course of the lives of others and sometimes of all mankind.

By your actions, deeds and thoughts you are going to make many lasting impressions. This is bound to happen, whether you want it to or not. It is up to you to decide whether the messages you send to others are positive or negative. As you go through your day, it will be good idea to give a little extra consideration and be conscious about how you speak and how you act. You may just be making an impression and leaving a legacy that will endure for generations to come.

Value Individuals

Be flexible and spontaneous and not always bound by plans and schedules. Schedules are important, but enjoying life and seeing it as an adventure is more. Be a courageous explorer, and venture into uncharted territory. Always have an image of confidence and excitement. Even when you are not sure about what is going to happen, be confident that it will be exciting and growth-oriented. Every day, discover new territories and make fresh contributions. This approach will empower you to navigate confidently even in uncharted territory, as well as evolve more rewarding relationships with others.

Putting people ahead of schedules and clarifying their expectations, even at the cost of some of our own time, is rewarding. Instead of comparing, competing, criticising or manipulating, try to be a person who is dependable, honest, direct, and keeps his commitments. Do not overreact to negative behaviour or criticism. Instead, be quick to forgive and do not hold grudges. Do not be judgemental. It never pays to categorise or judge others, as everybody works under different conditions. Be genuinely happy and try to facilitate the success of others. Generate a climate for growth and opportunities to get ahead. Learn to build on your strengths and work to overcome your weaknesses, if necessary with the strengths of others. Negotiate and communicate with others and separate the people from the problem. Focus on the other person's interests and concerns. Do not argue over positions. Be continually learning, read widely, and feast on the wisdom of the ages. Always be humble, listen to others and learn from experience. Be contribution-focussed and channelise your time and energy towards contributing rather than getting. Be service-oriented and seek to improve your quality of life, as well as that of others. The effort should be to produce extraordinary results. Do not burn the candle at both ends, try to continuously acquire new skills. Develop a healthy psychological immune system, so that you can handle problems confidently. A healthy immune system is essential for a happy marriage and a happy family, as well as for teamworks, groups, or organisations. Do not keep working till you drop from exhaustion. Do not spend till no credit is left. Do not persist ventures till you run out of time. Create your own limits for maximising your effectiveness. Focus on your work during times of peak energy. This will increase your creativity. Spend wisely, and save and invest for future needs. Lead a balanced life. Avoid not becoming a workaholic, religious zealot, political fanatic, crash dieter, food bingers, pleasure dieter, or fasting martyr. Be active physically, socially, mentally, and spiritually so that you can live more abundantly, confidently and securely. Your security should not come from work, associations, contacts, recognition, possessions, or status. It should come from within, from basing your life on principles, and living by your conscience.

Radiate positive energy and become more cheerful, pleasant, optimistic, positive and upbeat. Enjoy life more than what you have done so far. Never condemn yourself for every foolish mistake or social blunder. Do not brood about yesterday, and live sensibly and joyfully in the present. Carefully plan for the future, and flexibly adapt to changing circumstances. Develop a rich sense of humour. Laugh often at yourself, but never at others.

If you let go your earlier mistakes and lapses, you will experience a tremendous feeling of release. From that point, you can devote yourself to improving the quality of your life. Every breakthrough is a break with the past. All of us must discard the things that have been holding us back. These things prevent us from giving our best to society and to our respective organisations. We must follow the principle of first things first in our lives. When we pick up one end of the stick, we also pick up the other. Each follow-up of any principle has some consequences.

Check out things that are not first things. Free yourselves to work on first things first, while you abandon other less important things. Focus your time and effort on what is most important. Do not waste your time on rationalising. Do not burden yourselves with self-validation and vindication. If you do so, you will not feel free to respond to a sense of right and wrong. Make a commitment to simply respond to moral values. Try it, even for two weeks, and you will be amazed at the release of time and energy, which you had been spending on justifying action contrary to your conscience.

Do not feel unnecessarily guilty. Guilt coming from our own conscience is a great educator, as it helps us to know when we are out of alignment with the truth and with realities as they should be. But guilt out of a social conscience does not teach us much nor do most of us take it seriously. Life is a process of our learning from our mistakes, as well as our successes. "The only real mistake in life," said a wag, "is the mistake not learned from."

Our own basic sense of security should come from integrity.

Talk in the Other Man's Language

All of us face some crises at some time or the other. The best way to face a crisis is to learn how to prevent it from recurring. Many crises in businesses or in jobs or in personal life, result from failure to act until the problems become urgent. The result is that more time is required to do the job. For example, if you are behind schedule with the delivery of your book's manuscript, you can arrange to hand-deliver it. If you can't get something done on schedule, then find ways to adhere to the deadlines, such as by delegating tasks. Decide what you must do yourself, in order to gain time. Whenever such a crisis occurs, write yourself a note about handling it, to avoid similar problems in future. If you do not handle the problem or crisis early, it is likely to magnify and loom large on the horizon. Treat your problem like a punctured tyre which demands immediate attention on the road and cannot brook delay. If you delay changing it you are likely to be stranded. The same is true of handling a crisis. Learn to start early to overcome crisis. Similarly a health problem, like heart disease or fever, has to be given prompt treatment.

It is the early handling of a crisis which provides relief. Misunderstanding can cause delay due to improper communications. Periodic and timely inputs should be treated as a part of the early warning system. Other causes of failure are: not doing a follow through, and lack of supervision of delegated work. To avoid failure, one should always have contingency plans ready for alternative handling. It is important to analyse each crisis to devise ways to prevent a repetition of the same. By following the above strategy, you can save enough time and energy to deal effectively with cases in which circumstances totally beyond control make it necessary to push the panic button.

Tips to Help You Get Organised on Festive Occasions

In our country, hardly a month goes by when there is no festival being celebrated, whether it is the Independence Day (15 August), or Republic Day (26 January), or Deepawali or Dussera or the birth/death anniversaries of religious or political leaders. Some festivals call for celebrations, whereas others demand a serious or at least non-frivolous approach or observance. Some festivals are a matter of delight for children or younger people. Our effort should be to get as much fun out of festivals like New Year's Day or the festival of lights, Deepawali.

Make a list

Make a checklist of everything you and your family would like to do on any particular festival, such as making/getting clothes or giving a party or joining some religious celebrations or treating the kids to something they would like to cherish, or buying new items on an auspicious occasion. It is equally important to keep in view safety precautions in the use of crackers and other fireworks, so as to prevent fire hazards.

There is a theme for every season and hence it is important to decorate your office or place of work, keeping in view the significance or importance of the occasion. Obviously, the celebrations for a child's birthday should be different from those for New Year, or Independence Day or Republic Day, or Janmaashtmi, the birthday of Lord Krishna. It will be a good policy to pull out your tried-and-liked decorations from the past year if you have kept some decorations for recycling. If such items have not been preserved, you could start such a practice this year, so that the same can be used on later occasions. For instance, whenever any candles are left over from the Deepawali festival, I make it a point to store and use them when there is no electricity.

Find the festivities

Sometimes, you are not aware of festivities in your area on the important occasions. Local newspapers are the best means of finding out the same and you can, if you so desire, plan some outings for yourself and your family, and enjoy the season. Sometimes, the festivities can be as simple as a Mango Festival. All festivals ultimately get reduced to eating sessions. Plan your purchase of all treat items in advance, except for consumables. Indian festivals are a great way to keep in touch with family and friends. You can send greetings by post, or send e-greetings.

Search your TV listings

Quite often on festive occasion, TV channels bring out special programmes. If you are an avid TV watcher, search through your TV listings and make a schedule of all the programmes, cartoons, or plays, you and your family wish to watch. If the family is busy elsewhere, when a particular TV programme is aired, video tape it and watch it together later on. It is a good and a practical policy to organise treats into treat bags, in which an assortment of food treats is kept in each bag (this can be a polythene bag). This will ensure that every member of the family gets an equal amount of treats and does not feel discriminated against.

Organise a party

If you are planning to throw party at your house, plan for it ahead of time. Make a list of everything you plan to do, including the list of people you wish to invite. Be sure to send the invitations out early, preferably a few weeks before the event.

Get ready for parties you're attending

On festive occasions, it is usual to be invited to parties hosted by others. Determine in advance, what gifts you would like to present to the host. It is a good policy to never go to anyone's house on an invitation without a gift. It can be a bunch of flowers or even a book. Even a small gift will prove to be a big hit with the host – he will appreciate your thoughtfulness. If there is any doubt about whether the party is with or without spouses, nobody will take offence if you confirm the same are invited or whether it is an all male affair. It is always best to indicate in the invitation whether any dress code is expected to be followed. If so, you must dress accordingly.

Occasionally some friends get together and have a pot luck party. Every participant is requested to bring one item of food. If twenty people are planning to have a dinner, only two or three persons will be asked to bring one item for seven to eight persons. The item can be a vegetable dish or chapatis or rice. Twenty people bringing different dishes can turn such a party into a lavish feast. If any such party is planned on the occasion of a festival, find out what dish you will be expected to bring. Determine if it is an item, which can be prepared ahead of time, and then do so.

The spirit of the festival is lost, if you do not enjoy the festival and the company which you have selected to be with. Whether indoor or outdoors, enjoy yourself with your friends and neighbours, as well as the spirit of the festival with which your city might have been decorated. Take some photos or make a video movie to relish and savour the happy moments in the future.

Live Out of the Box

Decluttering is a continuous job. More so, when you want to organise your home. Organising a home quite often includes discarding or donating your clutter. One of the easiest ways to commence organising is to lessen your possessions. However, getting rid of things is often problematic for most people. It is one of the greatest challenges that people, wishing to get better organised, face. It is not so much a physical challenge, as an emotional one.

You can try the 'Living Out of One Box' method. When you leave your home, and stay in a hotel, you live out of only box or suitcase. You do not think of anything left back home. By nature we are hoarders most of the time. If an item is constantly in your sight, your attachment or emotions associated with it may interfere with your decluttering process. You may presume that you may need it some day and you let it remain. Anticipating its need, which may never arise, you just hang on to it. I noticed in my study over 50 VHS video cassettes which I had not used for the last five years. They were gathering dust and adding to the clutter. Like million others, I could not decide to get rid of them. My wife, on seeing my predicament just picked them up and sold them for not even a fraction of their original cost. I do not even remember what those cassettes were about and I do not miss them.

As they are now outside my vision, I do not even think about them. So if something is buried somewhere out of sight, you will most likely not even think of it. You can try an experiment by getting yourself a few suitcases. Select one room, which is full of stuff that right now perturbs you the most. Pack everything including "precious" and meaningful momentos or heirlooms or decorative items. Clear the room, as if you are vacating the house and moving out. Everything should be completely packed up in the boxes. Affix the day's date on the boxes.

Try to live the next two months without the articles in the boxes. When you need or want something, take it from the respective box, and use it. If you use any item at least once in two months, you can put it back in its appropriate closet, cabinet, drawer, countertop or shelf. After two months if there are still some items left in the boxes, which have not been used, it only shows that you have not missed them and they can be safely donated, sold or dumped. If you have not needed any item or thought about it in two months there is a very small chance that you will ever think about it or need it again. It may appear a bit difficult to live out of boxes, but this seems to be the only way to sift what you need from what is cluttering up your house and causing overcrowding in your limited living space. Keep in mind that the things you really want and need, will be out of the box and in their appropriate place within a few days. Never postpone what you want or have to do. Waiting for better times is a wasteful strategy, as at any given time, the time will never be just right. Don't wait to declutter. Simplify your life and find more time for the things you enjoy. Every time is a time to get organised!

How to Use the Telephone Smartly

Identify yourself

It is correct to identify yourself when you make a telephone call to anyone. Unless you do so, the person at the other end is justified in not divulging, if the person sought is at home, or busy, etc. When you have company and someone calls you up, keep the call brief, promising to call back later. It is impolite to have long conversations when somebody is sitting there waiting for you to finish speaking. It is equally impolite to use somebody else's telephone, without permission or for transacting business or making long distance calls. If it is something urgent, which necessitates your using his phone, ask his permission and offer to pay for the call.

Be polite

It is polite to answer the phone with a simple "hello". Remember that in these times, the less information you give out to those you do not know the better it is from the security point of view. There are a lot of companies soliciting business on the telephone. It is not impolite to hang up on such calls, after saying "No, thank you".

No calls after 9 pm

It is impolite to call at a residence after nine at night unless you have permission to do so or there is emergency or some other good reason, and you know the person well enough. If you are telephoning to invite someone to an event, let them know that right away, rather than first asking if they are free on a particular night. This avoids putting them in an awkward position of having to say no, after having said that they are free. Never forward a call to someone's residence, or give anyone's phone number without clearing this with them first. When using call-waiting, remember that the first call has priority. It is impolite to interrupt a conversation to take another call, especially more than once. If you have the call-waiting feature on your phone and you feel you must respond to a beep, do so quickly and graciously: "I have to answer this call. May I put you on hold for a second?" then tell the other caller that you're in the middle of a conversation and will get back to them. Return to the original person and finish your conversation without rushing. If you are indeed expecting an important call, let the person on the other end know that there is a chance you might have to cut the conversation short, in case that call comes.

Keep paper and a pen available

Keep paper and a pen beside your telephone and answering machine, if you use one. When you are listening to a phone message, a handy pen and paper will enable you to write all the details or points of the conversation you want to note, including name, telephone number and the points on which the caller wants your response or your views or reactions. I personally keep a diary in which I can note down the details of the messages and phone numbers from the answering machine. I do not save the messages. A written record of these is a better option. It enables me to respond even later on. It also saves me time, as I can respond at the time or moment that is convenient. Also when you speak to someone, you can jot down notes, so that you do not waste time trying to remember what the caller said and how you are expected to respond. You can also jot down important things that may emerge from the conversation.

Record your thoughts or points in advance

Before you make a phone call to anybody, write down your thoughts on the pad you have kept near your phone. Whenever you think of something you wish to tell someone later, record it in the phone pad or phone diary kept near the phone. You can call it a telephone diary. In fact, it is a good idea to jot down points before making calls. The presence of such a diary or note will also help you in giving your points if the concerned person calls. A diary or a pad near the phone is a good reference point when you absolutely do not want to forget what you want to say when you are talking to somebody

My mother lives 450 km from Delhi, in Jalalabad. I generally have a whole list of items written on my phone pad, about the things I want to talk about to her. When I call her, I am not at my wit's end regarding what I want to say to her. She also uses the same system and our conversation is meaningful. The system works beautifully.

Make use of an answering machine

If you do not like getting being interrupted by the telephone, while doing your important work, use an answering machine to take calls for you. If it is something very important for the person calling you, he can be requested through a prerecorded message, to leave a message for you. If the caller does not leave a message, it is obvious that what he wanted to say was not that important. Moreover, if you are sitting close to the answering machine, within hearing distance, you can listen to the message being recorded. So if you like you can speak to the caller right away. You have to simply pick up the receiver and start talking. If you don't want to speak to that person at that time, you don't have to. You can even choose whether or not to call him back at a later time, or call when it is more convenient. I use the answering machine extensively. It acts as my secretary, when I am out. Sometimes I find it full with messages. It can take 20 to 40 messages, depending on the size of the messages. I, download all the messages and numbers, and then delete them so that it can again receive messages afresh. It is my discretion to return all or some calls.

Leave a message for yourself
When there is something which needs my attention at home, and I am out, I call my home. My answering machine responds and I leave a message for myself. When I arrive home, a blinking light reminds me of a message. When I download it, I make a note of it, and so I remember what I wanted to do when I got home. Use of technology is one way of catching up with the developments in the world and improving your efficiency as well as regulating the utilisation of your time in an optimum way.

Minimise Clutter Throughout the Year

On the New Year or on festivals and holidays, sometimes life can be overwhelming, and hectic, because these days are often accompanied by a huge influx of new items like decorations, presents, and household items into your home. These items can add clutter to even the most organised dwelling. It is important to take steps to tame this clutter by establishing some useful habits. Some suggestions are as under.

Many times we are tempted to buy something as it looks good in the shop window. Make sure you really want or need any item before you buy it. Keep in view that if you own anything, you have to find room for it, clean it, maintain it, use it and eventually dispose it of. If you are still tempted to buy an item on an impulse, just note it down and give yourself a week or two before you actually purchase it. The waiting period will give you enough time to realise whether you really need the item or not, or you may even forget about it altogether.

- Decide where you are going to keep an item. Fix its "home" before you bring it home. Before you purchase

an item, decide how will you use it and where you will put it, once you buy it. If you buy something for which you don't have a place at home, it will add to the clutter. Put items away in their pre assigned place once you take them to your house. Don't just put gifts or new purchases "here, for now". Keep them in proper place right now, before they become clutter.
- Sometimes new items are purchased when old ones are still there. Adopt a policy of "out with the old, in with the new". I found that my wardrobe was cluttered with clothes. I have made it a policy that for every suit or shirt I purchase, I get rid of two similar old items. I have realised that if new items are brought into my life or my home, but none are discarded, soon I shall be overrun with clutter. To minimise this possibility, I suggest forming a habit of discarding one item each time a similar item comes into your home. For example, if you add a new video or DVD to your collection, get rid of the old one. Doing the same for clothes, children's toys, and kitchen utensils, will keep the clutter in your life and house under control.
- Go through all your belongings, whether in the entire house or in your wardrobe or in your personal library at least once a year. Even if you have been extremely careful about what comes into your home or what you buy or the gifts you receive, it is still easy for things, to pile up. For example, in every house, kids outgrow their clothes or get fed up with toys; or you may have lost some weight and now have clothes that are too big; or you might have put on some weight, as all of us do from time to time; or your tastes may have changed. Your hobbies or reading habits may have changed. Make a point to go through your closets, drawers and cabinets as frequently as you can or at least once a year, to make sure you are keeping only items that you care for or use. Since New

Year is often viewed as a time of new beginnings, you might consider doing this annual clear-out in January as a part of your New Year's ritual.

- Do not save items in the hope that you may need them some day. Think of that "some day" as today. If you do not have an immediate need for an item, no matter how certain you were that you needed it at the time you bought it, it is time to let it go, either in the form of a donation to a charity or giving it to someone who may actually need it. If you are not ready to part with the item, put it in a box and mark a date 3 to 6 months from now, on the outside of the box. If by that date you have still not needed it or used it, it is clutter. Find way that suits you to get rid of it, either by sale or donation or as a gift.
- Do not save items just because they have been gifted to you. Do not feel guilty if you get rid of a gift you don't like or use. Remember that the stress resulting from clutter, whether it is a gifted or purchased item in your home is far greater than the stress of letting it go. You will probably feel better by donating such an item, or giving it to a needy person. Let it serve a useful purpose elsewhere, instead of cluttering your home.
- Do not allow others to dump their extra or useless junk or belongings on you. If your friends or relations offer you their unwanted items, learn to say "no" graciously, unless you have an immediate need for the same. By the same token, don't turn your trash into someone else's clutter. Unless you are sure that someone really needs an item you're ready to part with, do not give it. Donate it to a charity rather than to an unwilling friend or a relative. In India, courtesy, rather than need, compels us to accept everything that is proffered to us. We must adjust to the changing times and, at the same time, hold on to the unchanging principles of good living.

The Home Office

Working from home is a dream come true for many and probably, also a compulsion for some. It has the advantage of allowing us to spend more time with our families while pursuing our profession. But working from a home office can also be very stressful, with family members competing for our time, attention and space, thus, making it hard to concentrate on the job at hand. One of the best ways to ensure that your home office or business is a success, is to create an organised office space, suited to your profession or your business. Here are some simple steps for setting up your home office.

Create your own space

With today's small houses or flats, space is probably the most important factor in setting up your home office. It is very hard to feel professional when your working area doubles as a dining room or children's study area or a general stacking place for books, grocery, stationery, or as a drawing room. An extra room in your house if available, should be the first choice for use as an office. If a separate room is not available, you have to create your own space. One way is turn a large closet into a workspace. If that is not available, you can use a storage bin as your office space or have a collapsible table to work on. Or you can block a corner of a room by segregating it with screens or heavy curtains. Due to the constraints of space, the important thing is to have a home office of any size, shape or set-up, as long as it serves your purpose. It is an adaptation which can be made even in a one room flat. What is required is creative re-arranging and using the limited area for optimum purposes. By organising your books, files and papers in vertical racks, you can use less floor space. Staying organised is what matters.

Decide what you need to succeed

Once you have carved out an office space, make sure that you have all the tools of the trade for your profession or job therein. It can be a phone or home computer or better lighting or writing material. Stock up material according to the available space and your budget. Do not clutter your small space. Everybody has his own method of working and you have to organise yourself accordingly. Staying neat and well organised in your office space will increase your efficiency. You will not have to struggle to find where you have kept things.

Get organised

Highly successful people take time to organise themselves. They are aware that it is extremely important to manage their time and have systems in place. In whatever way you may choose to organise yourself, it will help to clear your work place at the end of the day. Put out whatever you have to work on the next day, so that you can tackle it, as the first thing to be attended to.

Use your workspace for work only

In the home office, which may not be much of a space, the items which clutter up space like mementoes or photographs or anything which takes away the professional touch should be avoided. These things do not help you to work better. So, if you don't need anything in your home office, it need not be there. If some items make your home office a more comfortable place, let them remain by all means. As far as possible, the home office, should be off limits for the family during working hours, which can be flexible. It should be tactfully explained to the family members and their co-operation solicited. Devise your own ways of letting your family know when you must absolutely not be disturbed, such as when having a meeting with outsiders or receiving phone calls.

Be creative

Keep on trying to make your office space more productive and useful. It can be in making liberal use of the dustbin and using boxes and crates for putting your papers or files. There is no right or wrong way when you are working from your home office. If something does not work, try something different, till you get the desired results. It is only by trial and error that you can create a comfortable, well organised office space at home.

8
Preparing for Success

Succeeding is Easy

A quantum leap in life is possible only by continuous movement in the direction of excellence. This is the only way to reach a goal. It will be of immense help to us if we can identify and emulate the characteristics, qualities, traits and habits of successful people. Each person has his own methods for achieving goals. However, there are certain common habits or traits that can be associated with success. It is possible to achieve success by cultivating these qualities. The characteristics mentioned below are not all-inclusive. But they are all important ingredients for success.

Be enthusiastic and definite of purpose

A successful person is full of enthusiasm about whatever he undertakes. He is enthusiastic and passionate about his goals. A temporary setback does not diminish his zeal. He is eager to achieve more and more. His enthusiasm is infectious. Enthusiasm makes all the difference in his achievement. It also has a positive effect on the people working with him. A successful person always dreams big. He has a vision of success. And he makes sure that his vision does not remain only a dream. He transforms his dream into reality. He does all that is required to make that happen. A success-oriented person does not meander around aimlessly. He does not waste his time, lamenting that he has not achieved his goals. He is aware that nothing will happen unless he is focussed on a clear goal. Goals integrated with dreams spur him to stay on course. A successful person knows that action is more important than day dreaming. Many ideas occur to all of us. But they either remain in our thoughts or are confined to our day dreaming. Success-oriented people know that some action is better, than no action. God has gifted each human being with a brain. If a person does not act promptly, it is possible that the same idea may occur to others who may encash on it. A success-oriented person, despite facing adversity, hardship, opposition and setbacks, is persistent on his journey to success, to achievement of his goals. In fact he uses these obstacles as stepping stones, rather than stumbling blocks, to propel himself forward till he reaches his goal. He is convinced and recognises that defeat is a temporary phenomenon, and by persistence and hard work, he can overcome all setbacks.

A person working to succeed should decide that he really wants to do so. Most confusion is the result of indecision about the course of action to be adopted. Successful people know that any decision is better than no decision at all. Even a wrong decision can help in making adjustments, which can enable one to stay on course. Success requires a predetermined plan. The next step is to implement it successfully, in the required time-frame. Successful people know that they are capable of doing what they dream of. A person can achieve virtually any goal, as long as he has a clear vision of the goal, and persistence to last till it is achieved.

Successful people know what they want, and have a burning desire to possess it. They are focussed on the achievement of their goals. Success is nothing more than a predetermined plan. It has to be implemented successfully over a period of time. You can achieve any goal you set your heart on. The condition is that the aim should be clear. You have to match it, pursuing with your unfailing persistence long enough.

Faith

Success-oriented people always expect success. They believe that whatever be the odds, they will succeed. They have confidence in their abilities and ideas. Their faith helps them to remove all the limitations created by doubts, apprehensions and fear. They know that what they believe in will help in discovering ways to reach their goals.

Integrity

In the present climate in our country, many would argue that what matters most is success, and not moral character. People with lots of money and success tags, despite having a criminal record, are lionised in society. My answer is that like a tailor cannot transform a man beyond a certain limit, the tag of money cannot give permanent success. People may not call a successful man a crook, but they definitely talk about the underhand ways in which he won his success, if he has achieved the same through dubious means. Such a "successful" person will, sooner or later, suffer for lack of integrity. True success and respect cannot be achieved without integrity.

Surround yourself with achievers

Successful people surround themselves with other successful people. Winners serve as a support group, as an idea group to each other. They encourage others to succeed. They believe that there is enough room at the top. They are not jealous of the success of others. They do their best, everyday. They use powerful and pragmatic lessons and reach peak performance. They give their best to society.

Find out How Much Your Time is Worth

The first part of your focus on results should be to work out how much your time costs. This will help you to assess if you are spending your time profitably. If you work for an establishment or an institution, calculate how much you cost it every month, including your salary, taxes, the cost of office space you occupy, the equipment and facilities you use, the expenses on your administrative support, etc. If you are self-employed, calculate the cost of running your business for one year. To this figure add an estimate of the amount of profit your activity should be generating. A normal working person has approximately 200 productive days each year. If you work for eight hours each day, this will be equal to 1,600 hours in a year. From these figures, you can calculate an hourly rate, to get a reasonable estimate of how much your time is worth. When you decide whether or not to undertake a task, think about this calculation, to get a picture of whether you are wasting your own or your organisation's resources on a low yield task. Calculating the worth of your time will help you to work out whether it is worth doing a particular job. If you are spending too much of your time doing low-yield jobs, then it is time to either delegate or employ another comparatively less costly person to do such jobs.

Extracting Maximum Information from Facts

Start any proposition with the questions: when, where, why and how. You can solve almost any problem, like the launch of a new product this way. It will help you to get a clear idea of the implications of the solution to the problem you may have. Keep on asking these questions until you have drawn all possible information and inferences. Spend a lot of time in appreciation of any situation. These four words comprise a simple but powerful technique for extracting the maximum amount of information from a simple fact. While you may also reach the same conclusion without the use of a formal technique, a targeted appreciation provides you a framework within which you can extract information quickly, effectively and reliably.

Personal Goal Setting – Planning to Live Your Life Your Way

Goal setting is a traditional technique used by top-level athletes, businessmen and triumphant individuals in all fields. It gives a long-term vision and motivation. It focuses on your attainment of knowledge and helps in organising your resources. By setting goals on a regular basis, you make up your mind about what you want to achieve. This is the first step in moving towards the achievement of your goals. Goal setting is an established and recognised process for personal planning. The process of setting goals and targets lets you decide where you want to go in life. By knowing precisely what you want to achieve, you recognise, where you should concentrate. By setting sharp, clearly defined goals, you can measure, as well as take pride in the attainment of those goals. By setting goals, you also raise your self-confidence, as you recognise your intelligence, aptitude and capacity for achieving the goals that you have set.

We set goals on a number of different levels. For effective and result-oriented goal setting, you have to first decide what you want to do with your life and which significant goals you want to achieve. The next step is to break these down into the smallest possible targets, that you must accomplish for achieving your lifetime goals. Setting up this structure of plans, makes it easier to achieve your biggest life goal, breaking it down into easily achievable and less forbidding steps. Establishing lifetime goals gives you the overall perspective that has an effect on all other facets of your decision making. Only after your plan is finalised, should you start working, towards achieving it.

To have a broad, balanced coverage of all key areas in your life, you can set goals in some or all of the following aspects.

Attitude

Is your attitude positive or negative or is your mindset holding you back from progressing in life? Is there any part of your behaviour for which you feel sorry later? If so, you can decide to set a goal or goals to get the better of your problem by changing your attitudes.

Professional goals

What do you want to achieve in your career and in what time-frame do you want to work it out?

Family goals

Do you want to be a ideal parent and close to your children? If so, how are you going to be a good parent and bridge the generation gap? How do you want to be perceived by your family? What steps you should take to look after your family?

Financial goals

What financial position do you want to achieve in your life, and how much do you want to earn and by what age and stage? What steps you should take in this direction?

Physical goals

Are there any athletic goals you want to achieve, or do you want only good health even in your old age? What steps are you going to take in order to realise this goal?

Pleasure goals

What is your concept of pleasure? Is it money, good health, good company or fame? How do you want to enjoy yourself and your life? You should ensure you have enough time for yourself and your family. Once you have decided your goals in these areas, prioritise them from A to F.

Then review the goals in the key areas of your life and re-prioritise until you are satisfied that they reflect the profile of the life that you want to lead. Also make sure that the goals that you have set are the ones that *you* want to achieve, not what your parents, spouse, family, or employers want for you.

How to Achieve Your Lifetime Goals

Before setting any goals, it would be relevant to read good books and gather the maximum information on the achievement of your goals. This will help you to enhance the value and pragmatism of your goal-setting. Once you have set your lifetime goals, conceptualise a 30-year plan of smaller goals that you should accomplish for realising your lifetime objective. Have sub-plans for one, two, three, four and five years as well as six monthly sub-plans, which should progressively lead you to achieve your lifetime goals. Each of these should be linked and based on the previous plan. A daily to-do list of things is essential. Finally re-evaluate your plans from time to time to make sure that they fit in with the way you want to live your life. Periodically, review your long term-plans, and modify them to reflect your changing priorities and experience. This is the only way to stay on course. It is desirable to review and update your to-do list on a daily basis, so that you are not caught off guard.

How to Set Goals Effectively

The following broad guidelines will help you to set effective goals: affirm each goal as a positive statement, by coherently and positively expressing it. "Execute this job well" is a much better goal than "Do not be wooden-headed and make the same mistakes again".

Be specific, set a clear-cut goal. Inclusion of date and time would help you in measuring your achievement. If you can do this, you will know exactly when you have achieved the goal, and can obtain complete satisfaction from having done so. Where you have set several goals for yourself, prioritise each. This will avoid your feeling overwhelmed by too many goals, and will enable you to focus on the most important ones. Writing down your goals crystallises them and gives them more strength. Once your sub-goals and the main goal are clear, you automatically set priorities, which, in due course of time, becomes a habit.

Keep the objectives you are working for, small and achievable. If a goal is too big, it will seem, you are not making sufficient progress towards it. Keeping goals small and incremental gives encouragement and motivation. Your daily goals should flow from the larger ones. Set accomplishment goals, and not action goals. Do not set overambitious or vague goals. Set goals over which you can have as much control as possible. There is nothing more disappointing than failing to achieve a personal goal, for reasons beyond your control, like adverse business environment, faulty judgement, unsatisfactory weather, injury, or just a lopsided approach. If, however, you base your goals on your personal functioning, you can have some control over the achievement. This way you can conclude that you have reached the target by following your own methods and competence. Setting realistic goals, which you can achieve, is morale boosting. All kinds of people, including your parents, the media, society, even your servants or the nearest friendly shopkeeper can suggest improbable goals and ask you to achieve them. They will often do this in ignorance of your commitments, compulsions, desires and ambitions. For instance, when I took over as Director CBI, everybody began advising me, including my vegetable seller, fellow morning walkers and friends on how to achieve better results. It is also possible that you already have very high goals, without appreciating either the obstacles in the way, or the expertise you need to achieve them. Also, do not set goals too low. Your goals should be neither unrealistically high nor too low. Some people tend to set easy goals, they do not want to fail in their own self esteem. Your goals should be slightly beyond your immediate grasp. At the same time, they should not be impossible or so far off that there is no hope of achieving them. No one is even serious about achieving a goal that he believes is unrealistic. However, you may not be on sound footing in assuming that your goal is unrealistic. So you have to strike a balance in setting your goals. This approach will also help in reducing the stress and yet keep you fully preoccupied. When you have realised a goal, take the time to enjoy having done so. Appreciate the implications of the goal achievement, and continue your progress towards other goals. Reward yourself appropriately for the achievement of every goal This is the only way to be at your best, and be happy all the time.

Stress: How to Overcome It

Stress is the "wear and tear" our bodies experience. Stress occurs as we adjust to our continually changing environment and conditions. Stress has physical and emotional effects on us. It can make a person either positive or negative. A positive stressful influence can impel us to action, resulting in a new awareness, a new and exciting perspective of an issue or a problem. A negative influence can result in feelings of distrust, rejection, anger, and depression, which in turn can lead to health problems, including headaches, stomach upset, rashes, insomnia, ulcers, high blood pressure, heart disease, and strokes. Stress can affect our relationships with others. However, some stress is inevitable, when we have to adjust to different circumstances. Stress can help or hinder us, depending upon how we react to it.

How Can You Eliminate Stress from Your Life?

Positive stress adds anticipation and excitement to our lives. We all need a certain amount of positive stress to thrive. Deadlines, competitions, confrontations, frustrations and even sorrows can add depth to, and enrich our lives. Our aim should be not to eliminate stress but to learn how to manage it and use it to our advantage. It is negative stress which acts as a depressant and can result in our feeling bored or dejected. Excessive dismal stress may leave us "tied up in knots". What we need is to find the optimal level of stress which will motivate but not overwhelm us.

How Can You Tell What is Optimal Stress for You?

There is no single level of stress that is the best one for all people. We are individual human beings with unique requirements. As such, what may be distressing to one, may be gratifying to another. Sometimes, even when we are in agreement that a particular event is disconcerting or shocking, we are likely to be at variance in our physiological and psychological reactions to it. I had a batchmate who thrived on handling crisis after crisis. He felt stressed in a job which was stable and routine. Another colleague, who preferred stable conditions, felt stressed in a job in which duties were highly varied and more demanding. Our personal stress requirements and the amount we can withstand or endure before we become distraught changes with our age. A study has revealed that most ill-health is related to unrelieved stress. If you are experiencing stress symptoms, it is obvious that you may have gone beyond your optimum and healthy stress levels. The remedy is that you need to reduce the stress in your life and/or improve your skills to manage it.

How Can You Manage Stress Better?

Identifying unrelieved stress and being aware of it is not sufficient for reducing its harmful effects. Like many sources of stress, there are also many possibilities for its management. However, all methods require change. Change involves handling the source of stress and/or changing your reaction to it. The following suggestions can be usefully employed to tackle stress.

1. Become aware of your demanding, traumatic and worrying sources of stress and your emotional and physical reactions to the same. It will be helpful to write these down and also note down your reactions. Become aware of your distress. Do not adopt a policy of paying no heed to it and glossing over your problems. Be clear about which incidents, events or persons distress you. What is the significance and implication of such events in your life and career. Ascertain how your body responds to the stress. Do you become jumpy or tense or worried or physically upset? If so, in what precise ways do your reactions manifest themselves?

2. Identify what you should or can change and whether you can change your stress inducers by avoiding or eliminating them altogether or reducing their intensity or shortening your exposure to them. Handling such situations or managing them over a period of time, instead of on a daily, weekly or ad hoc basis, is one of the best ways to tackle them. Another way is to take a break or be physically away from such sources or premises. All this requires time and energy. Here, techniques like goal setting, or goal rearranging or time management and delayed gratification strategies can be helpful.

3. The stress reaction is caused by our perceptions of threat—physical, professional and/or emotional.

Minimising the intensity of our emotional reactions to stress leads to the lessening of the stress. Another useful approach can be, not to view your stress inducers in larger-than-life terms or treating a delicate situation as a calamity. Expecting to please everyone and overreacting and viewing every thing as absolutely crucial and urgent can be another source of unending stress. Putting things in the proper perspective and taking life as it comes is the best way of destressing. Put any situation you face in life in the proper perspective. Do not brood over the negative aspects of any problem. Do not become a slave to "whats and ifs." Do not believe that you are to be on the centrestage in every situation. Make every effort to perceive the stress as something you can cope with, rather than something that will overpower you.

4. Train yourself to moderate your physical reactions to stress. Slow, deep breathing generally brings the heart rate and respiration back to the normal, and relaxation techniques can reduce muscle tension. Other suggestions for reducing tension are building your physical reserves and doing moderate, prolonged rhythmic exercises like walking, swimming, cycling, or jogging, eating well-balanced, nutritious meals, maintaining your ideal weight, and avoiding nicotine, excessive caffeine, and other stimulants. Mixing leisure with work, taking breaks getting enough sleep and being consistent about your sleep schedule will also help. Pursue realistic goals which are meaningful to you, rather than goals that others, like your family, have for you. In any endeavour, some frustrations, failures, and sorrows may cross your path. Instead of finding fault with yourself, always be kind and gentle with yourself and be your own best friend. Some mutually supportive friendships/relationships can stand you in good stead in tackling crises.

The Power of Success

Many people have asked which is the best time and best method to prepare for success and get ahead in life. In fact you have to actually prepare for that. Like everything in life success does not just happen. If you want to improve your status in life, you have to take action. This is a great challenge. You can have more than you have at present. You can become more than you are. I have discovered that my income seldom exceeds my personal competence and personal development. Once in a while you may be lucky and earn more. But unless you grow, your income will go back to the original level. A writer has said if you take all the money in the world and divide it among everyone equally, based on their competence and dedication, it would soon be back in the same pockets. However, you can have more by becoming more. Unless you change yourself, you will remain what you are at present. You should be prepared to take a risk. Doing things you haven't done before will always be risky. But there is no other way you can have a fulfilling life. Leap out of the comfort zone and take a risk. Be excited about the possibilities for the future and be grateful that you have the guts to take action. If you want to become more, or do more with your life, be prepared to make changes and improve your own self. Pool your resources, undergo courses, and get the support you need so that you carry your dynamism, into whatever you want to do or accomplish in life. Coping with your life and the changes therein, make sure to take action today, to create order out of chaos as well as a happier and healthier workplace.

The high road

Using adversity and setbacks to renew your commitment to your aspiration and making the most of any situation are the hallmarks of a victor. Realistically, not giving in to depression no matter what life flings at you can be tough. But a winner needs a strong mind, heart, soul, and a strong character. This approach means making personal sacrifices, overcoming fears and self-doubts, and withstanding the objections and criticism of others. This also entails integrity to be honest about yourself and your choices in life. While we may make big mistakes in our life, we should refuse to let our past dictate our future. Instead, we should believe that every day gives us a fresh chance at happiness. We should also acknowledge that we have only ourselves to blame if we are unhappy with our lives. Instead, take the responsibility for your choices and your life. Keep in mind what Elbert Hubbard said: "One machine can do the work of fifty ordinary men. No machine can do the work of one extraordinary man." It is up to you to be extraordinary.

Always move on the high road of life. The low road or low approach can never make you happy. Do not choose to be miserable in the midst of abundant joy which life has to offer. Never believe, even for a moment, that nothing and no one can make you happy. Only settle for the best. Never settle for less than you deserve. Never be complacent that what you have is enough. Be brave and take the high road, in your life, which has countless opportunities for happiness. So be valiant and choose to be a winner. Decide to make yourself count to have a meaningful life and live it to the full, with your whole heart and soul, and with uprightness. In short, choose intelligently. From time to time, it is essential to do some introspection to break out of the rut and overcome self-defeating beliefs which keep people trapped in a pattern of unhappiness and disappointment. Such an exercise, will enable you to discover which choices are you not making in your life and which actions you should take to turn your life around. It will also enable you to discover what is keeping you from making such choices and taking positive action, and what steps you need to take to improve your position. Remember the instances in your life when you made your dream come true and how elated you felt. The idea behind the introspection is to repeat the same experience in other area of your life.

Always be a Winner

What is the difference between a winner and a loser? The kind of happiness you get in your life depends on the type of person you are, or the type of person you are committed to be. Anthony Robbins, a famous writer, says: "Goals are a means to an end, not the ultimate purpose of our lives. They are simply a tool to concentrate our focus and move us in a direction. The only reason we really pursue goals is to cause ourselves to expand and grow. Achieving goals by themselves will never make us happy in the long-term. It is who you become, as you overcome the obstacles necessary to achieve your goals, that can give you the deepest and the long-lasting sense of fulfillment."

It is a fact that in the same set of complicated circumstances, two persons will assess and react differently. One may choose to wallow in misery and upbraid life for his disasters. The other may perceive the same difficulties as a challenge that he can, and will overcome. It all boils down to which path you choose. It is all a matter of choice. A pessimist sees himself as a victim. A sceptic feels miserable and lets others be conscious of it. He also makes others miserable too. Be accountable to yourself and your life, even if it is difficult. But taking responsibility for our lives enables us to grow as human beings. We should have enough self-respect to admit that we have made a mistake. We should also have enough guts to look at ourselves and our life with forthrightness. Of course, it needs courage to face up to our shortcomings and failures. Instead of blaming life for your misfortunes, strive to make the best of a bad situation. The strategy, however, should be that you do not settle for less than you deserve or are capable of. Do not presume that your past will always determine your future. If this was so, no poor but intelligent and hardworking person would ever achieve anything or any position in life. Basically, never presume, even for a moment, that you will never have what you want out of life. Do not use past failures as indicators of the way things are going to be and of the way things are supposed to be. If you are using past failures as alibis for your future failure, your happiness will always seem to be out of reach. In this state, you just want things, and wait for happiness. But at the same time, you don't believe that you have the power to create it. This approach will keep you trapped in a prison of your own making. You can break out of this self-defeating sequence by taking responsibility for your life. Take further step by identifying that you want more out of life and that you have the power to make your dreams come true. You can do this by rebuilding your wavering self-confidence one day at a time, one significant step at a time. Start by improving, just one area of your life and keep enlarging it from there.

Keep on encouraging yourself to simplify your life. One good reason to work at simplifying one's life is the joy that anything uncomplicated generates. Simplicity adds to transparency. It also leads to fearlessness and innocence. It gives you powers which only a liberated state can give. It makes it possible for us to live, not merely as pale and diminished version of oneself. It also enables us to live with a new and an expanded mind. It is for us to decide about the conduct that will be the measure of our lives. It is a fact that sometimes unforeseen things, beyond our control happen, despite our setting goals and planning. But if what happens is "not-part-of-the-plan" you have, you still have the rest of your life. By this approach, you can have both freedom and power. Freedom is actually more glorious than power. Power is about what you can control and freedom is about what you can unleash. Whether we like it or not, we have to cut the ropes that bound us. We must constantly strive to improve and excel.

Abraham Lincoln used to say: "I always take the time for preparation. Give me six hours to chop down a tree and I will spend the first four sharpening the axe."

Break Free from Old Ideas

Some suggestions for doing the same are as under.

Admit it when you are wrong

A highly creative person is not willing to stick to any one stand for life. A fluid, flexible and adaptive mind is not rigid. A creative person is not like those who spend all their time trying to prove that they are always right. Some people spend all their mental energy in stonewalling, bluffing, blaming and denying. A positive and creative person admits it when he is wrong, strives for a solution of the problem or difficulty, and proceeds to the next step. Only non-creative and diffident people think that it is a sign of weakness to say, "I made a mistake". The fact is that such a statement is actually a sign of maturity, personal strength and individuality. Creative people are not rigid and are not afraid to admit that they have changed their minds. It is astounding how some people get into, and stay in, a sticky state of affairs only because they are reluctant or afraid to admit that they've changed their minds. A creative person, on getting new information or on finding that he feels differently about an earlier decision, does not hesitate to accept that he has changed his mind. He does not let anyone or anything push him into a corner. If a decision does not serve his best interests, in any given situation, he will have the strength and courage to "cut his losses". He will not hesitate to change his mind and then get on to higher things. It is always open to each one of us to demolish narrow thinking patterns and become more creative. Always be prepared to admit that you are not perfect, and we can make mistakes. This is an indication of intelligence and courage. If a new information comes to your notice, and so warrants be willing to change your mind. Most of what we know about our business or profession today will be revolutionised completely in the future. We should be willing to adapt. The highest intelligence lies in recognising an opportunity and encashing it.

Organise Your Work and Home Life

After my retirement from the Government service, I am overwhelmed by the seemingly endless torrent of paperwork, e-mails, ideas that occur to me, the things I want to do and the books I want to write or interesting news items on which I want to comment. I want to keep track of so many things, but I file them away and then forgot about them as something more pressing comes up. I have tried to make lists of all the things I want to do. For extra busy people, I have put together some ideas which can help in getting their life in order and keeping their sanity.

Some of these are: take notes; keep a small notebook and pen handy wherever you are, to enable you to jot down ideas or appointments or things to do. Instead of trying to remember such things later on, let your diary do the job.

Telephoning: Some people talk endlessly on the telephone. They hold you up and jam telephone lines. It is better to set a time limit for each phone call. Politely communicate this to your caller by asking if he has any other point to discuss. Thank him in a way as if you are now ending the call. If any points are being repeated, you can tell the caller that you have noted this point earlier. Whenever you get a telephone call and you are in a hurry or want to finish the conversation, tell the caller so. Be business-like on the telephone. This way, you can save yourself the stress of trying to end the phone call. Help the caller by condensing the information you want to give. Be precise and to the point on the telephone.

Spend time wisely while waiting: Use the waiting time at a doctor's clinic or dentist's clinic, at the airport or railway station, before a meeting with your boss or any other waiting time, to catch up on reading, or use space time to tidy up, or for filing or other tasks, at your own place.

Give and take help: Be sure to thank and praise a subordinate, co-worker or member of the family for any help rendered or other efforts made on your behalf. Such appreciation will encourage them and they will be happy to help you when you need their services again.

Do not procrastinate: If you delay any work, you will only get stressed out when you think about it. Your mind will blow it out of proportion, to the extent that it will then become almost impossible to finish it. Make sure you first tackle the work that's already piling. Dividing your work into manageable segments will make it easier. Delegate what you cannot finish due to the paucity of time. Get somebody to help you, either on reciprocal or payment basis. Save time and labour by collecting all similar work to be done at the same place or in the same direction or requiring similar efforts. If certain things are to be done in a room in your house, then do them all together. Similarly complete all market errands at one go. It will save time and avoid numerous trips. Make a list of stops while planning your outing route. You can stop at each place along the way and get some work completed or done, so that you can accomplish more in less time. Go through any old unneeded files. Try to keep free space in your filing system. Use sticky notes to write errands or other tasks to be done and stick them prominently on the door or on your table to remind you of the things to be done.

Schedule some time for fun: Always include some personal time for yourself, whether it is taking a leisurely bath or listening to music or watching a movie or doing anything which entertains you. Out of 24 hours, you deserve some time for yourself.

Once and only once: You should handle each piece of paper only once. Read it and dispose it of by either filing it, redirecting it to someone else, scheduling it in your programme or tossing it in a dustbin. Do not add all kinds of paper to an ever increasing pile on your desk in the hope that you will dispose it of eventually. Use any system which jogs your memory. Most of us waste too much time everyday just searching for things. Have a system that works for you and your lifestyle, and apply it to your day-to-day routine. Use this system consistently and regularly. You will discover time slots you thought you never had.

Dedication Begins at the Beginning

If you want to manage your time better, the first step is to ask yourself the question: "Exactly what are my goals?" Take a sheet of paper. List your personal lifetime goals, including the things you would like to look back upon with satisfaction in your old age. The goals should be specific, like acquiring an educational qualification, saving enough money for your old age, a home of your own, or maintaining good health or a good figure, or a certain weight or a working knowledge of either a foreign language or some other of your own country's languages, if more than one language is spoken in your country.

Next list your professional goals, like reaching the top position in your profession, or attaining a specific position in social, official or political circles. Do not be vague and aim for just general things like a higher salary, or a promotion or greater prestige. Focus on specific targets like a salary of a certain amount, promotion to a particular job, or election to a specific office. Also list your short-term goals, the things you would like to accomplish in the next six months, like acquiring a new set of clothes, or learning a skill like music or dancing or mastering computers.

The goals should be specific and attainable. They have to be the things you really want and are willing to work for. Remember, all goals are subject to change at any time. The list should reflect your best judgement of what you would like to accomplish. Any changes in the goals should be based on realistic changes on the ground. Frequent changes in the list can be both upsetting and unsettling. Analyse your lists. Do not be upset if the list includes more things than you can do. Assign priorities to the various tasks and jobs to be done. Select six most important goals in each category. Write them down at some place where you can see them everyday. Memorise them. One of the best places to remind yourself is to keep the list under the glass of your table.

At every opportunity, ask yourself, "Is what I am doing now moving me closer to my goals?" If the answer is *no*, then plan to have some of the less important jobs delegated to someone else. You can even downgrade in priority some jobs to be accomplished in your least productive time. You must learn to say "no" to the good so that you can say "yes" to the best. If you are discouraged, just remember that the darkest night has never been able to obliterate all the stars.

Plan for the day

There is no greater waste of time than unstructured, unfocussed, poorly planned and poorly managed meetings. If you are in a position to hold meetings, keep this in mind. Ask yourself whether the meeting is a substitute for action. "Can I make the decision myself?" Then ask yourself, "Is the meeting a ruse to share the responsibility or to postpone a decision?" If a discussion is a must, use a telephone and conference call facility to save everybody's time. Don't meet unless you have to. The amount of time wasted like this is staggering if it is multiplied by the number of people in attendance.

Success is the Best Medicine

A successful man never imposes limitations on himself by questioning whether he will succeed or not. A successful man looks at the problems facing him as opportunities to learn and move forward. A successful man makes a commitment to himself to do his best. On this subject, it has been rightly commented by W. N. Mury: "Until one is committed, there is hesitancy, the chance to draw back, always ineffectiveness. Concerning all acts of initiative and creation, there is one elementary truth, the ignorance of which kills countless ideas and splendid plans; that the moment one definitely commits himself, Providence moves too. All sorts of things occur to help one that would otherwise, never have occurred. A whole stream of events issue from the decision, raising in one's favour, all manners of unforeseen incidents and meetings and material assistance, which no man could have dreamt would have come his way." A successful person is aware of the fact that only when he is serious and committed, he will achieve his objective. The very desire to achieve unlocks his genius and all his energy to achieve his definite aim. It is only the decision to achieve which leads to achievement. He then does whatever it takes to succeed.

To be successful, you have to learn to enjoy what you are doing or are required to achieve. Doing well is a reward in itself for a success-oriented person. We should form the habit of working for the love of work, and get involved. The only road to success is through clear purpose. The *Bhagavad Gita* rightly preaches that your right is to the action, and not the results. A man with a success-oriented attitude is happy, and likes doing what he does. Failure hurts. But it is more hurting when failure comes your way when you do not give your best. Things improve when we ourselves improve. There is no magic wand to make things and circumstances better. It is a fact of life that despite your doing your best, sometimes you cannot eliminate failure and disappointments. Doing your best itself is rewarding and boosts your self-respect. You have to be persistent to succeed.

Calvin Coolidge had said, "Nothing in the world can take the place of persistence. Talent will not. Nothing is more common, than unsuccessful men with talent. Genius will not. Unrewarded genius is almost a proverb. Education will not. The world is full of educated derelicts. Persistence and determination alone are omnipotent. The slogan 'Press on' has solved and always will solve, the problems of the human race." Persistence is the main input to success and winning to anything one undertakes. Thomas Edison, the inventor of the electricity bulb and the gramophone said: "Genius is one per cent inspiration and ninety nine per cent perspiration. I never did anything, worth doing by accident, nor did any of my inventions come by accident. They came by work." Another great achiever said, "If people knew, how hard I have worked, it would not seem, wonderful at all". According to Carlyle: "A man with half volition, goes backwards and forwards, and makes no way on the smoothest road; a man with a whole volition advances on the roughest, and will reach his purpose, even if there be little wisdom in it ... The man without a purpose is like a ship without a rudder .. a waif, a nothing, no man. Have a purpose in life, and, having it, throw such strength of 'mind muscle' into your work as God has given you." A firm purpose is at least half equal to the deed itself. Success lies in the constancy of purposes.

Make Time Work for You

You should be an active participant in real life dramas. Face whatever comes your way. You will be criticised, even for doing the just and correct things. Your best defence should be the armour of indifference if you have done your work to the best of your ability. It is a very effective shield against even the most biting and sarcastic criticism. Even in the face of the most bitter criticism, never lose your zest and enthusiasm for life. The creative power of enthusiasm can do wonders for you. Being enthusiastic leads to good health. Depressive thoughts affect optimism, faith, and lifestyle. The only way is to be enthusiastic, and act enthusiastic. It is the same for courage. You can be courageous, just by being courageous and overcoming your fears. Forcing yourself to be happy, will make you happy. You can get ahead in life only by being enthusiastic. Never minimise your work or the opportunities that come your way. Never berate yourself and your work. Enthusiasm is a good indicator of the quality of life you lead. Avoid giving way to annoyances, or showing irritated reactions. Take things as they come. Be urbane and philosophical. Accept the problems that come in your life. But, at the same time, discover the best possible solution to overcome them. If one door closes, another opens – this is a reality in everybody's lives.

Do not waste time on the closed door, or the method which has not yielded dividends. Lamenting does not yield results. Instead, find another door or method to solve your problems. You should be clearly aware of the resources and the opportunities that are available to you. Treat problems as opportunities. See the best, in every situation. Expect the best at all times. Destiny calls each one of us, everyday. Everyday can be a great day if you do not waste time in futile recrimination. Never even think of, "If only I had done ... this or that." This reminds you only of past failures, bad judgements, and mistakes, which are best forgotten. Failures and thoughts of failure should be cut out of your life. Expect the best at all times, even in the worst of situations. Cast out of your life all negative expectations. Embrace the positive. Cast out the defeatist concepts or suppositions. Remind yourself that you are better than you think you can be. Clem Stone says: "Millions of people, in every walk of life, have never tried to achieve high goals that were solvable. Why? They were told or believed, 'It can't be done'. They never learned, or applied the essence of the art of motivation with a positive mental attitude. It could have helped them achieve any goal. In the quest of achievement, we should not violate universal laws, the laws of God and our rights. Write down your goals and concentrate on them. Study, think and plan strategies for half an hour or more daily on your goals, or difficult problems. If only such people had motivated themselves to recognise, relate, assimilate, and apply from what they read, heard, saw, thought, and experienced. The subconscious will come up with the answers through repetition, repetition, and repetition."

Most of us are aware that the time available to us in life is limited. However, it is simply a question of the way you look at life. One has to give up a range of activities as one grows old, due to slow reactions and depleted energy. All of us get old. E. M. Foster writes, *"The people I respect most behave as if they were immortal and as if society was eternal. Both assumptions must be accepted, if we are to keep open a few breathing holes for the human spirit."* If we feel and act that life is eternal, we will always have time for everything we want to accomplish. It is a paradox, true that it is the busiest person who has time for every aspect of life and its several activities. All of us can make time available by proper planning. It is up to each one of us to decide how we regulate and utilise our time. Next to being available is the ability to cultivate the habit of happiness. It is this which forms an outgoing and generous personalities. One should not only be a loveable person, but also a loving one. Love and warmth should be a part of your life. Allied with it is the quality of being trusted. But it does not come cheap. You can underscore your integrity by the way you live. It would ultimately lead to better and greater productivity. It will enable you to work towards achieving the goals of your organisation, rather than focussing on trivia.

The image of victory is within you

It is essential to form good habits. In my view, the number one good working habit is to clear your table or desk of all papers except those that relate to the jobs at hand. The second important habit is completing the tasks in the order of their priority and importance. The two valuable abilities that we must acquire are: the ability to think, and the ability to do things, in the order of their importance in our life or the programme for the day. When there is a problem facing you, your effort should be to solve it then and there, if you have the necessary inputs to make a decision. Don't procrastinate and keep putting off decisions. You have to learn to organise, depute and supervise. We rarely get tired when we are doing something interesting and exciting, especially if it is in accordance with our inclinations. If you act as if you are interested in your work and your job, ultimately the act will become a fact, and your interest real. It will also reduce your tensions and your worries. Relax whenever you can. Let your body relax and go limp. Try to work, as far as possible, in a comfortable position. An uncomfortable body position results in aching shoulders and fatigue.

Observe yourself four or five times a day to find out whether you are making your work harder than it actually is. Check up whether you are using muscles that have nothing to do, with the work you are doing. This will help you in forming and developing the relaxation habit. Ask yourself, at the end of the day, whether you are tired. If you are, is it because of the work you have done, or because of the way you have done it? As long as we do our work with poise and an unhurried attitude, properly balancing labour and rest, maintaining at the same time a simple faith, our duties will be lightly borne and done to our complete satisfaction. If we add worry and anxiety, the spell of calm and peace will be broken. Tension creates and adds to stress and strain. Any element of panic, even in a small degree, destroys the power to relax, both mentally or physically. The man who worries, will always be dragged down. He cannot go forward. The man of action will march ahead of others. Men who act just do so, without bothering about anything. If they are worried about getting things done, they would never be able to deliver the goods.

Always Carry the Image of Victory Within You

You must identify your goals. The following suggestions will help you in this direction.
1. Identify your aim, objective and purpose in life.
2. Write down your aims and goals and set a definite timetable for reaching them
3. Choose goals that are consistent with your perceptions and the way you see yourself.
4. Break your goals down into easily achievable sub-goals and objectives.
5. Review your goals from time to time. Check your progress. All your efforts should be to make your dreams come true. Make your goals a reality.
6. Constantly set a new goal after you have achieved one.

You should have different types of goals, that is, short-term and long-term goals. Long-term goals are the things you want to accomplish either during your lifetime or in a span ranging from one to a few years. You should know where you ultimately, want to reach. You can break down your long-term goals down into one or more short-term or intermediate goals. These could include the tasks you want to do during the next year or few months. Always balance your intermediate goals against your long-term goals. You can further break down your long-term and intermediate goals into short-term or monthly and weekly goals. The idea behind this approach is to enable you to move towards your target. Make a strong, irrevocable and irreversible commitment to give it all you have, and all you are to achieve your goals. It should also include having a strong commitment to yourself to reach your full potential as a human being.

For achieving your career goals, the following points are a must and should be kept in view all the time:

1. Keep away from time killers and time wasters. They may be your colleagues, relations or friends. Avoid negative thinkers and people who are always moaning with a negative approach.
2. You should know your present job inside out. Become an expert at it. Your objective should be to be the best man for the job you are doing. You should become so competent in your job and indispensable that your employer will look to you for any troubleshooting. Always make efforts to be more organised and orderly.
3. You should become the one person who can take on any job, including those not wanted by others. You should build the reputation of a go-getter, who can complete even irritating tasks that have been hanging for few months. Whatever job comes your way, it should be completed in the best possible way. Do not be a person who is content to do just enough to get by. Your objective should be the maximum performance, so that the best results are achieved.
4. The top man always wants to know what is happening in his organisation. Keep your boss well posted with information about your work and accomplishments. Instead of complaining about things which may be wrong, you should make a suggestions for improvement.
5. You should not discuss problems regarding your family or your colleagues, subordinates or superiors.

9
There Is More than One Way to Success

Use Will Power

The way to succeed in life and achieve your goal is to start sooner, work harder, and know more than anybody else. Losing is a habit and so is winning. You can cultivate any habit by persistence. You should not accept defeat as final, at any cost. Defeat is only a temporary setback. You should also remember that anger and aggression do not move a person to tears. But an act of kindness would. Your willpower and strength of character can build what force may destroy. The secret of breaking a bad habit is to replace it, with a good one. You must spot the habit you want to shed. Nobody really wants to acquire a bad habit. Bad habits have a way of sneaking up on us, when we are not on our guard, or are careless, or inattentive. For breaking bad habits, it is essential to use strong willpower, rather than "wish power".

You should reward yourself when you achieve even a small success. This also includes even a small dent in breaking a bad habit. If sometimes you slip up during the process of forming a good habit, there is no need to belittle or berate yourself. As human beings, we are apt to fail. Sometimes it may also be that our method of correcting ourself has failed. There is nothing wrong in taking failure head on. Breaking a bad habit is more difficult in the initial stages. But it is not an impossible task. Those wanting to change themselves and their lifestyle have to put in a lot of effort.

You should keep your mind active all the time. This approach will automatically deter wastage of time by keeping your mind on your aim. If you have a problem you can't solve, go through all its aspects before you go to sleep at night.

Have the Determination to Succeed

If you think you are beaten, you are,
If you think, you dare not, you don't.
If you like to win, but you think you can't,
It is almost certain you won't.
If you think you'll lose, you are lost,
For out in the world, we find that
Success begins with a fellow's will
It is all, in the state of mind.
If you think you are outclassed, you are,
You have got to think high to rise,
You've got to be sure of yourself, before
You can win a prize.
Life's battles, don't always go,
To the stronger or faster man,
But sooner or later, the man who wins,
Is the man WHO THINKS HE CAN.

If you are determined to succeed, you can devise your own success creed. You should write down such a resolve, in a place and put it where you can see it frequently and regularly. You can ask your family to share it. Your creed should emphasise your belief in yourself, and those who work with you, your employer, employees, friends, family, and God

Almighty. Believe that God will lend you a helping hand to succeed if you do your best to earn it through faithful and honest service. Believe in prayer and proclaim, *"I will never close my eyes in sleep without praying for divine guidance to the end."* Believe, and be patient and tolerant with those who do not believe as you do. Believe that success is the result of intelligent efforts. It does not depend on luck or sharp practices or double crossing your friends, your fellowmen or your employer. Believe that you will get out of life exactly what you put into it. Believe that you will be careful to behave with others, as you would want them to behave with you. *Do not slander people you do not like. Never slight your work, no matter what you may see others doing. Render the best service you are capable of. Pledge yourself to succeed in life. Remember that success is always the result of conscientious and efficient efforts. Forgive those, who offend you because, sometimes you will offend others and you may need their forgiveness.*

If you want to know whether you are going to be a success, in your business, or any other profession, ask yourself, whether you can organise and control your time. If you cannot, you will surely fail. Time is as important as your life. It is a luxury to have enough time – time to play, time to rest, time to think things through, time to get things done and know that you have done them to the best of your ability. The only way for this is to take enough time to think and plan things, in the order of their importance. This way, your life will take on a new zest. You can add years to your life as well as add more life to your years. You should not accept the power of adversity over you, if and when you face it. In this way, you are not denying adversity but its power over you. A combination of positive thinking, goal setting and visualising success, can certainly lead to successful outcomes. The factor of belief is fundamental to all success.

The Successful Person's Secret Weapon

A successful person likes to be effective. To be effective, he builds trust. The best way to do that is to always keep the promises made. This is not a revelation. It is worthwhile to reflect on why so few people respect their promises to get back to you with their reply, quotation, orders, report or anything else. Unless they are your subordinates, most people, whether in business or even in Government, do not deliver on their promises. This can be seen from the number of assurances given in the Parliament or by the Government. Such people and such organisations, do not realise that the "trust" element in their words and their credibility goes down the drain if they do not deliver what they promise.

When people lose their credibility, others, who know about it, avoid them. Such people are considered untrustworthy, and their reputations get tarnished. If such people have their own business, the business is bound to be adversely affected. The question is: Why do people over promise or underdeliver? From what I have seen, most people make promises verbally. They do not write the details of the work to be done, so that they can remember to follow up. If we write down our promises, there is no chance of forgetting! It is a simple fact. Research shows that a normal brain has on an average 40,000-50,000 ideas daily. Due to sheer volume of ideas, it is not possible to remember them all. So it is best to jot down any promise made, or any idea on which action is to be taken. A daily diary or planner, with space for writing any notes, follow-ups and things to be done is a good device. A diary is an important tool in accomplishing your role and responsibilities. A loose-leaf ringbinder system with two pages per day one for appointments and the "to-do list" and the other for scribbling notes, is generally the best. You can use any system that suits your needs with additional accessories such as notepads, business cards and goal sheets. These can be very useful although they are only part of the organising solution. Some disorganised people have the feeling that electronic organisers are the best tools ever invented. To effectively plan your time, your activities, your appointments and to make sure you keep your promises, a paper system is more convenient and perhaps most effective. I tried using digital diaries, but I found that I had to spend double the time to operate them. First I had to record, what I wanted to do and later delete the same. Though I use my digital diary, I have realised that a paper system is simpler and can be kept right in front of your eyes as an open document, compared to electronic organisers such as the Palm Pilot, Casio or HP and Psion, where one has to make sure that data does not get lost due to a wrong command or a dead battery. I use an electronic diary for storing contact details and a few other functions. Choose whatever system suits you best, since you are the one who has to work in this system and no one else. More than the tools, it is the use of the tools to achieve your targets that is important.

Increase Uptake of Oxygen for a Better Life

Oxygen has been called life, life's breath and the basis of life. Actually it is a colourless, odourless gas, which makes up 21 per cent of the Earth's atmosphere. Most forms of life, that is human beings and animals, require it as a fuel. It provides for the metabolic "burning" of foods, to produce energy for a process known as aerobic metabolism. Human beings get oxygen from the air through their lungs and into the blood. Oxygen binds itself to the red blood cells and travels throughout the body.

The body's ability to carry and use oxygen is called oxygen uptake. It is an indication of cardiovascular fitness and resistance to disease. When a person is overweight, generally out of shape, and leads a sedentary life, his heart, lungs and blood system may struggle to meet the body's demand for oxygen. Lack of cardio-respiratory endurance can have the following effects.

A person may tire easily. He can become short of breath, with just a minor exertion. The pulse will be fast. It will be above 80 or 90 beats a minute. Deficiency of oxygen will force the heart to beat faster and work harder for pumping blood, throughout your body. Lack of oxygen can cause muscles to lose strength.

You can improve oxygen uptake in the following ways: any form of moderate exercise or physical activity will create an increased demand for oxygen. Regular cardiovascular workouts or even walking, for even 15-30 minutes daily will help train your heart, lungs and other muscles to absorb oxygen from the blood more easily. Such exercise generates better flow of oxygen. In turn, this will boost your energy and stamina. The exercise may be moderate, but it should be non-stop (aerobic) exercises. This will force your muscles to demand a continuous supply of oxygen to burn the energy stored in their cells. Within a few weeks, the exercise will have the effect of forcing your body to use oxygen more efficiently, leading to the strengthening your heart, lungs, blood flow and virtually every system in your body.

This is called cardiovascular fitness. This fitness will boost your energy and give you overall good health. The exercise will also fight and control obesity, diabetes, hypertension and high blood cholesterol, and will give you a better quality life. The exercise should be done regularly and not less than five times a week for not less than 30 minutes per day. It should be done at a comfortable pace and yet be vigorous enough to sustain a moderately elevated heart rate, but not so hard that it makes you short of breath or tires you out. The correct level of exercise and training should always be kept in view.

For overall fitness, it is desirable to quit smoking. Carbon monoxide in the blood from cigarette smoke competes with oxygen for space in your bloodstream. Thus, it restricts the body's access to oxygen. When a person stops smoking, his blood can again carry a healthy supply of oxygen throughout his body to help it function better.

Many things can be done at an aerobic pace. Some people find hiking, walking, jogging and swimming more interesting. These are natural and comfortable exercises. Some people prefer indoor machine workouts on a treadmill or an exercising cycle. It is again a matter of personal choice. If you prefer sports, you can alternate among tennis, basketball, soccer, skating and cycling. Aerobic exercise will make a difference in the way you feel, strengthen your heart muscles and lower your resting pulse. It will help the heart to pump more oxygen-rich blood with each beat, thus giving a healthy heart which is the basis of all activity in life! Unless you have good health and are able to do hard work, any amount of planning and contemplation will not produce the desired results. Good health is imperative for doing well in any sphere of life.

Let Bygones be Bygones

If you have made mistakes in the past, why should you waste your time brooding and worrying about them now? If you regret making them, there is nothing you can gain by thinking about them. How many incidents of the last year, which appeared to have wrecked your life, do you remember now? At that time, they appeared to be the biggest calamities which could befall you. Now, with the passage of time, they appear, at worst, unpleasant memories, or have been totally forgotten. Sometimes, we inflict more suffering on ourselves by trying to remember. Bury the past and forget about it. That's the best thing to do. You should exclude from your mind everything which depresses and troubles you. All of us, at one stage or the other, have committed sins, both against man and God. The same have already taken a toll on us. Why not put the unpleasant experiences behind you and out of mind? There is no benefit or advantage, in brooding over past mistakes, blunders or humiliations or misfortunes. Remembering them can only cause more mental harm and unhappiness. Painful and distressing memories or old ghosts are a useless menace, dragging us down and retarding our progress. Every day should be a new day with a fresh start, minus all those old ghosts or worries which upset us. All of us face disagreeable situations. We should not allow them to make us permanent regrets.

There is no fixed method of getting rid of old ghosts and unpleasant memories. Many things have happened to all of us which we would have preferred not to have happened. Sometimes we do not want to talk about them. They have one utility and lesson for us – we should leave them but not cry over spilt milk. After this utility is over, the only sensible approach is to bury them deep and blot them out of our memories. You should neither castigate or nag yourselves, for any unpleasant happenings in the past. If you have done your best to accomplish a particular thing, and still something adverse has happened, take it in your stride. Try to improve matters in the time to come. Forever talking about it and regretting it, will take more out of you than physical injury. You should start each day on a new slate, with the resolve to profit from past mistakes. For making the most out of our lives, we should erase from our life everything which upsets us, makes us anxious and worried. First take disagreeable things out of the way. Deal with the tough problems as the first things in the day. Solving these will boost your self confidence and give you a feeling of achievement. Your day's first resolution should be not to waste a single minute on worry. At no cost, don't ruin your peace of mind. Priority number one should be to bury old regrets, grievances, and the imagined and real slights. Do not allow them to rule and ruin your life. Vexations, pinpricks, annoyances and perplexities should have no place in your schedule. Remember, that today is the day that counts. The habit of brooding over the past and looking back is fatal, for efficiency as well as peace of mind. What is over, is over and is done with. When you finish your day's work, you should also lock your office troubles and worries, there itself. Make your home, as far as possible, out of bounds for office or business worries, anxieties or discussions. Your home should be for enjoyment and peace. Do not use it for wear and tear on yourself over past problems or potential worries. Your home should be a place for rest and rejuvenation, where the entry of worry or anxiety or jealousy or anything that is offensive and disagreeable, is banned. All disagreeable and painful things, appear much worse than they actually are. At night trifling annoyances get magnified into insurmountable problems. We spend one-third of our life sleeping and resting. Let this period be used for this purpose and not for remembering past regrets or imagined grievances. Your home should be a power house. It should supply all the replenishment, energy, strength, and courage you need. It should be a place where you renew and revitalise your confidence. You should not make your home, or your working place a stale place. A stale place and a stale environment will produce only stale results. Your home should be a place where you can sharpen your mind and make it vigorous and fresh.

Use Your Skills to Succeed

The mind is like a bow. It you keep the bow stretched and strung for long, it will lose its throwing power. So keep it fresh. Use your home to cheer yourself. Worry will wear you out more than any amount of work. It is the biggest enemy of efficiency and success. Effective work is possible only with mental harmony. Form the habit of calming down, relaxing mentally and physically in the fortress of your home. By hurrying or fretting over any task, you cannot do it faster or more efficiently.

Says George Wharton James, *"Worry takes our manhood, womanhood, our high ambitions, our lawful endeavours, our daily lives; it strangles, chokes, bites, scares, hanging on cliff, sucking out our life blood, draining our energies, our hopes, our aims, our noble desires; leaving us torn, empty, stricken, hopeless and despairing. It is the nightmare of life which takes the good out of us, that takes from us all the nutritious juices of our body."* However, it is up to us to neutralise our fears, worries, anxieties and all such enemies. They are not only the enemies of efficiency, they also drain away our lives. The antidote for these enemies is, harbouring only such thoughts which are the exact opposite of those that depress you. You will then reverse not only your mood, but also your lifestyle. Thoughts of courage and determination, will drive away worry and fear. In the same way, love will drive out hatred and jealously. The choice is yours. You can choose a worry-free life and a lifestyle which can lead to achievement of all you desires. Remember to hug those you love at every conceivable opportunity. It creates a feeling of peace and happiness. It is a very special gift that everybody finds pleasing. It is a gift which only you can give. The person you are hugging, gives it back to you. It requires no special training, no equipment, or agility. So every day is a perfect day to show your hug-ability.

Always Keep Smiling to Have a Perfect Day

Everybody can learn from others. Nobody is perfect. A pleasing personality is always attractive. The following emphasises the value of a smile. "It costs nothing, but creates so much. It enriches those who receive, without impoverishing those who give. It happens in a flash and the memory of it sometimes lasts forever. None are so rich, that they can get along without it. And none so poor, that they are not richer for its benefits. It creates happiness in the home, fosters goodwill in a business.

"It is rest to the weary, daylight to the discouraged, sunshine to the sad and Nature's best antidote for trouble. Yet it cannot be bought, begged, borrowed, or stolen. For it is something, that is no earthly good to anybody, till it is given away."

Most people hate following rules because they cramp one's style. Take time to write a set of your own rules and try to live by them. You can make your own rules, the way it suits you. It is better to have some rules, rather than none. The following rules are suggested.

1. The most important is to have self-respect. Don't let anyone humiliate, demean or insult or denigrate you. If somebody does, don't let him get away with it. This will make you more confident and enhance your self-respect.
2. Never be afraid to speak up for the cause you feel is right. Never be afraid to express your opinion. You will regret it later if you do not speak up. But at the same time, be aware of your limitations.
3. Have time for contemplation and thinking. Learn to spend time alone, doing whatever pleases you. It could be reading or writing or reflecting. Do not waste time on the things which do not matter.
4. Listen. But never believe everything you are told. Have your own acid test for doing the right thing and judge it for yourself.
5. Never let your conduct be ruled by others' expectations or the desire to please them. Act in accordance with your basic values and conscience.
6. Be alert. You can learn a lot by keeping your eyes and ears open. Quite often, it is more paying to keep your mouth shut!

7. Reserve your judgements. Don't always judge a person by what you see or hear them do. Appearances can be deceptive. Be more understanding.
8. Have a good word for everybody. If you don't have anything nice to say about anyone, don't say anything at all. Pay compliments only if you mean them. This approach will make you popular. It will make people think twice if they want to say anything nasty about you. Follow your instinct and intuition.

Structure Your Rules

Nobody reaches the top, without slipping up. When someone stumbles, give him a chance. It is maximum goodwill and minimum friction that are important. A successful person establishes clear achievable objectives, for himself and his organisation. He finds ways and means to reach out to, and touch, everybody in his team and organisation. In any job, you will find a number of so-called experts. Do not be overawed or bewildered by them or their data. More often than not, your own judgement is better, than that of the experts. You may be presented for driving people towards a high performance, standards, and expectations. It should not deter you from setting high standards and goals. Ultimately, everybody likes to win and become a winner. You will be respected as a successful leader if you help others to attain greater heights for a worthwhile objective. As an individual dedicated to achieving success, you have to devise your own rules and guidelines for successful living. During the course of the day, you may come across a number of ideas for efficient working. The problem arises later on when you want to recollect and act upon them. You can devise your own mode or manner for storing and recalling them, whether it be in a notebook or in a computer or a pad memo. Do not be afraid of mistakes and misjudgements. It is experience which leads you to victory.

Plan for a Better Tomorrow

Temporary setbacks to the achievement of goals should not lead you to despondency. It should be regarded as a transient phenomenon. There is no question of permanent failure. Failure hurts everybody. But it can also make a positive contribution to our lives, if we learn to ask ourselves the question: why did I fail. It has to be answered honestly for rectifying the situation. In situations like this there is a tendency to look for scapegoats and blame somebody else for our failures. An honest self-examination of failure can help you improve immensely. It can be a turning point in your life. The honest answer can turn all your ventures into success and catapult you forward. Having failed and reached the bottom, there is no way to go, except upwards. Failure will also free you from risks, because there is nothing left to lose.

A person who is always doubting himself cannot be a great doer. Doubt and fear of failure are the greatest enemies of mankind. They have played havoc with the humanity and will continue to do so, if not checked. Always remind yourself that the creator has created you for success and victory in life. You are born to be a winner. All the emphasis in your life should be to make your mind and personality positive, creative and success-oriented. Never give into discouragement. It will undermine your ambition and dull your desire to reach the top. One act of discouragement and self-doubt will demolish what you may have painstakingly built over years. What you have set your sights on can become a reality with a positive attitude maintained over a period of time.

Negative thoughts lead to discouragement. Discouragement will never lead you to success. For winning in life, you must develop a winning attitude. Assign yourself the role of a conqueror. It cannot be over-emphasised that not only success, but also prosperity begins in the mind. You cannot achieve success and prosperity with a beggarly mentality. Your moods and thoughts should always generate courage and hope. Your personality and bearing should advertise success, confidence and faith. Never mar your mood and life by anticipating disagreeable experiences or misfortunes, which might never occur. If you take stock of your life, you will notice that most of the disagreeable and unwelcome experiences, expected in the past, did not actually happen. If at all they did, they were so late in arriving that they had lost their sting. You really did not suffer half as much as you expected. The events did not turn out as badly as anticipated. Instead, you had an excellent life, full of success. Remember, you cannot escape your own estimate of yourself. Your performance and image cannot be better than what you model yourself on and what you think of yourself. Your own model is what your faculties try to reconstruct and produce. You cannot rise above your own conviction of yourself. Always carry a lofty and high image of yourself. The world is not interested in the weak, ineffective and self-deprecating man. It wants strong heroes and models it can emulate. Saturate your consciousness with lofty and noble ideas about yourself. Imagine yourself without imperfections, defects and deficiencies.

Suggestions, whether from outsiders or from ourselves, affect our thinking. Keep out of your mind that which you do not want happening in your life. Always concentrate on success, health, and prosperity. Constantly, keep in front of you the image of the person you want to be: noble, firm, effective and honest. The model you carry in your mind will make you what you want to be. Our own vision of ourselves either takes us to the top or down to the abyss. Never harbour thoughts of inferiority. Regard yourself as a "Man of Destiny". Do not let anyone denigrate the image you have of yourself. A perfect person can emerge only out of a perfect model. It is exactly in the way, a sculptor sees his model in an uncut rock.

Michelangelo could not have made the best sculptures of the world, without first creating the same in his mind's eye.

Stop Fuming and Fretting: Kick Off for Success

Procrastination is not just a harmless habit. It is anathema for a successful person. People fail in business because they procrastinate in making decisions. Marriages fail, because couples keep putting off decisions that affect their life and marriage. Procrastination is not germane to human nature, but an acquired trait. Neither is it an incurable disease. It is a bad habit. Like all bad habits, it can be changed and broken. Clutter and procrastination go hand in hand. One thrives on the other. Both can overwhelm if not tackled promptly and quickly. You can devise your own methods for dealing with them. You can prepare a list of things to be done. Write notes to yourself as a reminder of the things to be done, in a descending order. You can even talk to yourself and persuade or direct yourself to do the things which matter in your life and profession. You can order yourself, for instance, and say, "Mr/Ms ... you are not going to leave the office without accomplishing so and so task (name the task) and completing the incomplete jobs ... (name the jobs here)".

Fixing deadlines and making them known to yourself or your team is another method of accomplishing the maximum. You can also adopt the technique of dealing with the difficult problems as the first thing in the day. There is always a great temptation to put off an unpleasant or difficult task. But a successful man or woman first tackles the most difficult task at hand. This approach gives a feeling of accomplishment. The notion of doing things perfectly paralyses many people. This does not lead anywhere. Perfection is only a comparative matter. There is no end to it. The rewards of achievements are far greater than the rewards of procrastination. The breaking of the chain of procrastination not only gives you satisfaction in your job but also all round happiness, eagerness, zest and productivity. A successful person does not run down himself. He concentrates on the talents that God has given him. He tells himself repeatedly that he can do a good job. He prays for God's help and grace, and does not hesitate to help others. He forgets his own problems by helping others to solve theirs. He adjusts his self-image towards victory and happiness.

Successful Managers

Across the world, managers face constant challenges and hence, some of them show signs of business burnout. Many suffer from "Priority Problems". Put simply, they make the error of attending to the urgent rather than the important tasks. Some of these people function for exceptionally long hours, with no time for themselves or their family members or other people in their lives. Their working methods are disorganised, affecting their communication skills. This results in difficulty, in communicating effectively with their team members as well as their families. This situation can have an enormous impact on their own morale and productivity as well that of their teams. Their situation on the home front can be even worse. This is the result of not paying enough attention to the priority problems. All one has to do to improve one's life is to emulate what successful managers do.

1. Highly successful executives are splendid and distinguished role models. They put into practice what they insist on.
2. Highly successful managers invest time and money in their team and in themselves. They develop their people and themselves through education and coaching.
3. Highly triumphant managers are methodical. They know how to control their time. They have arrangements in place which enable them and their team to work on crucial issues.

4. Highly successful managers take care of their health, so that they are fit and healthy. They recognise that only a healthy mind and body can improve efficiency and general happiness.
5. Highly successful managers make time for their personal lives. It is a priority because they appreciate that it makes them happier and more successful.

You can put these tried and tested secrets into action. Learn to get your priorities right about people, work and home to enjoy a longer and better life.

Simple Secrets for a Successful Life

1. *Prioritise your life* – Determine what's most important to you in life. Put it down on paper, and in your heart.
2. *Write down your goals* – Look at them daily. Prioritise them in the order you want to accomplish them.
3. *Write down your plant of action* – With written goals, note down what you must do to achieve them. Set completion dates. Act on your plan. Make it happen.
4. *Read about successful people* – This will help you determine an ideal life for yourself.
5. *Consult achievers* – Show your goals and plan of action to someone who has achieved them and ask for advice. Why reinvent the wheel?
6. *Never settle for less than the best* – Do not compromise on things that are most important to you. You get what you settle for. Settle only for the best in life.
7. *Learn from others' mistakes* – It's cheaper and less painful than making your own.
8. *Focus on what you want* – Not on what you don't want. You get what you focus on.
9. *Make others feel important* – With a compliment, hug, fax, letter, e-mail, gift, and most importantly, your valuable time.

10. *Health is the most important* – Achieve and maintain excellent health. Only with good health can you enjoy your wealth!
11. *Do what you enjoy* – While benefiting all concerned. That's it!
12. *Relax, be at peace* – Be calm and peaceful, so you can act appropriately and wisely under most situations.
13. *Get plenty of rest* – To recharge and energise your body and spirit.
14. *Drink lots of water* – To cleanse and lubricate your system. This also helps to keep your skin moist and youthful. It's the best beverage.
15. *Travel more to experience more* – Broaden your horizons. Learn how others live. Be adventurous to enrich your life.
16. *Take risks to move ahead in life* – Especially when you have little to lose and much to gain. You'll learn from many new experiences which will add to your outlook of life.
17. *Learn something new daily* – This is the secret of happiness. Notice that when you are learning something you want to learn, how happy you are!
18. *Aim for excellence in all things* – No matter what job you are doing or what profession or business you are in, aim to be the best. The better you get, the better you are. Keep improving.
19. *Constantly improve* – A little gain daily is better than no gain. Do this in all areas of your life. Never stop!
20. *Use a computer* – To organise your life. Master it so you can be more effective in all you do. You'll be amazed at how much it can help you grow and bring out your natural talents for increased creativity.

21. *Develop speed for productivity* – Challenge yourself to achieve faster, yet with less effort and money. Be effective!
22. *Success is a journey* – Not a destination. Always keep this in mind. It's the gradual progression towards your goals that's important. Enjoy the journey.
23. *Don't compare yourself* – Especially with others! There will always be people who achieve more or less than you. Why discourage or frustrate yourself? Do your best, that's good enough. Period.
24. *Build a reputation of integrity* – This is all you really have. Build it on integrity, honesty, and being reliable. Be patient, it takes time. It's well worth all the effort.
25. *Make your life memorable* – Simply do things that are important and memorable to you. You will be in total control.
26. *Enjoy a simpler life* – Specialise in making your life a work of art. You are the artist. Life is easier when it's simpler. Make your life a masterpiece.
27. *Spread kindness worldwide* – Those who display it least, often need it most, especially these days. Be always kind.
28. *Exercise daily* – Walk for at least 30 minute daily, alone or with a good companion. Use it to enjoy nature and to clarify your priorities and goals.
29. *Eat healthily* – Visit natural food stores. Read books about eating healthy. Talk to healthy people. Learn so you can live to be a glorious 100 years old.
30. *Reward yourself* – Set daily goals in the evening for the next day. Determine a reward for yourself after you accomplish your day's goals. Make them reachable and challenging for each day.
31. *Smile first, it's contagious* – Smile at people you meet. Be friendly and appropriate. Give a smile to someone new daily.

32. *Think 'win-win'* – In all situations, for all concerned. When the world thinks and acts this way, we will have world peace. Let it begin with you.
33. *Read more to learn more* – On subjects you enjoy. Make time for it. You'll be amazed how much this will benefit you and others.
34. *Set a great example for others* – For others to emulate. Be the best you can be and inspire others to do the same.
35. *Live life to the fullest* – Make every second of your life count. Fill your life with joy, pleasure, bliss and giving.
36. *Make a difference in the world* – You have a lifetime to contribute to the betterment of the world because you have lived. How will you contribute? Do it now.
37. *Have more fun – more often* – Enjoy what you are doing now, the next hour, the next day. Look at each situation as a lesson in life. Have fun in learning from each situation, no matter what it is.
38. *Be forgiving to all* – So you can forgive yourself. Then keep moving on with your life, without burdens.
39. *Contribute to others* – When you contribute to other people's lives, you also contribute to your own.
40. *Inspire yourself* – Make your life a miracle of happiness.

10
New Year Resolution

The year comes to an end and with this we close another chapter of our lives. For some, the last year was a great year. For others, it was not. The New Year means a chance to make a fresh start, on a clean slate, hence, a new beginning. Whatever may have happened in the last year, we have a chance to begin anew. What changes will you make in order to make the New Year the best year ever? My computer sometimes gives troubles. When I am working, it often tells me that have performed an illegal action and hence the programme will be shut down. Obviously, it does not approve of my handling of it, because I may be cluttering the drive or not pressing the right button or overtiring it. The same is true of life, getting cluttered, like hard drives with files or software that we don't need or use.

If we are not careful, and do not "delete" these undesirable components, we continue to leave them installed on the "hard drive" of our lives, making our lives cluttered, beyond an acceptable level. This built-up clutter inside us has an adverse effect on our physical and mental systems. We just leave it there, giving all kinds of reasons to justify doing so. We often do the same with computers. When the computer hard drive crashes, the space is cleaned. The useless clutter on the hard drive disappears. If I have to use the computer, then I have to reload the software I need. But at least the system has been cleansed, and will run efficiently to the optimum of its capability. Similarly, when we eliminate clutter like old junk, rusted machinery, clothes, ill feelings, grudges, and the emotional baggage that we carry, our personal "system" will be cleansed too. It will run more efficiently. Wipe your slate clean and begin the New Year with a renewed sense of excitement and gratitude to and about your life. Tony Robbins says: "The past does not equal the future." The most important thing anybody can do at any given time is to achieve the maximum and best results.

You do not have to continue the same pattern of living and doing the things that have not taken you to your goal. Life is not lived in quicksand. Remind yourself, the definition of insanity is, "doing the same thing over and over again, and expecting different results". If you want the New Year to be different from the last then you have to plan accordingly. You have to decide what you expect from the New Year. Decide for yourself what actions you will take to obtain the desired results. You also have to decide what kind of person you will shape yourself into, to make that happen. Decide about the qualifications you will need to upgrade your skills and whose help you are going to enlist. The New Year should be a mirror for you to see what track your life was running on and whether any change is needed. It doesn't have to be that way all the time As you reflect about the last year, you will fondly recall a few wonderful things that happened. Then, decide on the changes that you want to make in your life in the New Year. It is best to list as many things as possible, to make the New Year the best year of your life. Try to pen down anything that occurs to you. Write down at least ten goals, the achievement of which will give you happiness and a sense of fulfillment to make the New Year the most memorable year of your life. Commit yourself to your goals and decide on the changes and strategies you would like to adopt to achieve those goals, so that when this year ends and another New Year comes, you will be able to look back with peace and satisfaction. Doing well is itself a reward.

Self-Improvement Books from Sterling

ISBN 81-207-2730-4

ISBN 81-207-2711-8

ISBN 81-207-2710-X

ISBN 81-207-2401-1

ISBN 81-207-2049-0

ISBN 81-207-2446-1

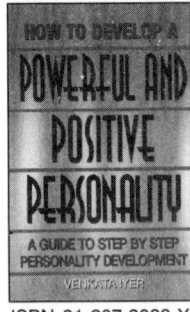
ISBN 81-207-2089-X

ISBN 81-207-2136-5

ISBN 81-207-1859-3

For Complete Catalogue write to

Sterling Publishers (P) Ltd.
A-59, Okhla Industrial Area, Phase–II, New Delhi–110020
E-mail: info@sterlingpublishers.com   Website: www.sterlingpublishers.com